The Sales Winner's Handbook:

Essential Scripts and Strategies to Skyrocket Sales Performance

Published by:

DFD Publications
215 East 95th St.
Ste. 31G
New York, NY 10128

"In comparing the number of new business meetings for the period of January through June 2007, to that of the same period in 2008, the results are quite remarkable. Our Junior Brokers achieved an increase of 51% in new business meetings with prospective clients, resulting in a projected increase in total revenue of $1.1 million."
Peter Hennessy, President
The Staubach Company

"Working with you over the past two years has had an enormous impact both on our sales team and on our sales revenue. Our total sales increased by 32%.... We couldn't have done it without you..."
Marlene Vogele, Vice President Sales
Gateway EDI

"My new sales were up 23% this past year, and I am extremely happy with the outcome. You have made me feel more confident about myself and my ability to sell."
Kathleen Henry
Mitchell Printing & Mailing

"Now, more than ever, Wendy's no nonsense, methodical results-oriented approach will yield consistent results for all sales organizations.
Andrew Mullen
VP Sales, Americas, Expand Networks

"Real actionable advice I would recommend for today's sales professional."
Sanford Brown, Chief Sales Officer
Heartland Payment Systems

"Members of our sales team have repeatedly found your insights to be highly impactful, no-nonsense and immediately applicable to their daily prospecting strategies. It's easy to tell which of our reps leverage your tools most often ... they tend to be the ones who book the most business!"
Mary Bittel, Marketing Director
American Slide Chart/Perrygraf

"In the four years I have been the CEO of ParishPay, we rarely have had someone impact our organization and improve our results as you have. Last year we had three inside sales staff members and this year we have two. Our results this year were 128 appointments set by phone in 3 months, as opposed to 45 last year. If anyone can do math, they can see the value of your input in a phone-based sales operation."
> Andrew Goldberger, CEO
> ParishPay/InTuition

"[Wendy] ...totally revolutionized the way I speak with prospects. ...I needed a new elevator speech and the information from the call helped me to create it. Last evening, I went to a networking event where I used my new elevator speech for the first time. What usually happens for me at an event like this is that I see people's eyes glaze over and I end up going home frustrated with no leads. Last night, ...people actually listened to what I had to say and I went home with four strong leads, one of which has already turned into a request for a proposal."
> Ed Navis
> SPHR

"I recently called six companies and was able to get four solid introductory appointments on my calendar with minimal effort! If I can keep up this pace I can make more money in less time."
> Tracy M. Brodd, Account Executive
> American Identity

"I was able to reduce the amount of objections and increase the appointment closing ratio.... Yesterday I was able to secure three appointments in one hour by practicing your methods."
> Ken Galanaugh
> DSI Solutions,Inc.

"...since your workshop, my team is consistently scheduling more and more new business appointments. By applying your techniques, I, personally, am nailing two to three appointments an hour!"
> Chris Whiteside, Business Sales Manager
> Sprint

"If it wasn't for Wendy Weiss I wouldn't have half the leads I do. I'm definitely seeing results."

Brett MaslinAdams & Company Real Estate
Adams & Company Real Estate

"After having completed a mere three coaching sessions with you, all of the members of this canvassing pool are setting record numbers of highly-qualified appointments with high-level decision-makers"

Marti Hendrickson, Executive Managing Director/
National Sales Manager
Newmark & Company Real Estate, Inc.

"We have reached new heights this year. We have been able to get into so many new accounts and it is no coincidence that we are closing more accounts this year."

Steve Stolfi, National Sales Manager
CT Corsearch

"Wendy's cold calling tactics are well thought out and they work - something she was able to validate early on. And they are easily duplicable... She is a very quick read and was able to learn all about our business early on - allowing her to ask the right questions, determine our needs and actually show us the solution that would meet our needs."

Sheril Hirsch, Director, US Sales Leadership
Avon Products, Inc.

"No one can arrive from being talented alone, work transforms talent into genius."

Anna Pavlova

Table of Contents

Part IV.
When Your Entire Sale Takes Place Over the Telephone

Part V.
In Conclusion

Acknowledgements

I am very grateful to the many people who encouraged me and assisted me with this project. I would never have written The Sales Winner's Handbook without their assistance.

I owe a special thank you to Michael Johnson of SalesDog.com who motivated me to write this book. I must also thank him and Tina LoSasso of SalesDog.com for their help in marketing this book.

Thank you, thank you to Karen Dennis who patiently read and reread and reread this book and is responsible for the copyediting, lack of typos and the easy-to-use flow.

I also want to thank Marlene Vogele and Tamara Hancock for their support and many great ideas (that we have been able to implement) for this project.

I want to thank all of my clients; I have gained in wisdom and knowledge from working with you.

Lastly, many, many thanks to anyone and everyone that I have ever cold called in my entire life.

Introduction

All sales people use scripts.

Many sales professionals claim that they never use scripts and never would. Many take issue with the entire idea of scripting, saying that scripts are "phony," "don't work," "make you sound like a telemarketer," or that "every call is different so it's impossible to use a script."

The reality is that all sales people use scripts. Here is why:

You probably hear certain questions from your prospects over and over and over and over. If you've been in sales for even a very short time, you probably have fairly standard answers to those questions. If you are more or less repeating the same answers every time you hear particular questions, those answers are your scripts.

You probably also hear the same objections from prospects over and over again, and have developed fairly standard responses to those objections. If you are responding to a particular objection over and over again with more or less the same counter-argument, those responses are also scripts.

You also probably have a fairly standard way you introduce yourself to new prospects. Sometimes this is called an 'elevator speech' - a brief introduction you could make to a prospect in an elevator that would be finished and understood by the time the elevator reaches your floor. If you have been in sales even just a little while, you are most likely repeating, more or less, the same 'elevator speech' over and over again to prospects: by another name, this is a script.

You see, it doesn't matter that your consistent responses are not written down or that there are slight variations in the way you deliver them each time. If you are repeating the same language with different prospects or customers over time, then you are using scripts.

The question is *not*: should you use a script?

The *real* question is: does your script work?

Does your script work to get you the results that you want?

And if it does not, shouldn't you be saying something else?

If you are calling prospects to make appointments, does what you say get you the appointment? If it doesn't, your script doesn't work.

If your entire sales process happens over the telephone, does what you say get you the sale? If it doesn't, your script doesn't work.

If you are making prospecting calls to schedule appointments and you are in fact making many appointments, why would you ever want to say anything other than what works?

And if your entire sale happens over the telephone and you are in fact closing many sales, why would you ever want to say anything else?

> **...all sales professionals use scripts; not all sales professionals use good scripts.**

Sales professionals who are extremely successful have scripts that they use regularly and that they have honed over the years. They know what to say and know when and how to say it. Many of these successful professionals do not think of what they are saying as a script, but if you pay attention you will hear them use the same introductions, talking points and responses over and over again. The really successful sales people are not winging it.

Bottom line: all sales professionals use scripts; not all sales professionals use good scripts.

This is why I have written *The Sales Winner's Handbook: Essential Scripts and Strategies to Skyrocket Sales Performance* - to give you access to effective, proven scripts that work.

Part I of *The Sales Winner's Handbook* is on *Cold Calling in the 21st Century - The New Rules.*

When I started my business 20 years ago it was fairly easy to get prospects on the telephone. Not so many sales professionals were cold calling. There were not as many ways people could be contacted, and prospects were less irritable and much more receptive. Today things are very different. Cold calling still works: however, you need to know the rules for *Cold Calling in the 21st Century.*

Part II is on *Gatekeepers, Voice Mail and Email.*

20 years ago the only challenge to reaching your prospect was the occasional gatekeeper. Today calls are screened by caller ID, voice mail *and* human gatekeepers. Your emails can be trapped in spam filters. Prospects are busier, more stressed and less accessible than ever before. In this section you will find scripts for dealing with human gatekeepers; a formula to create effective voice mail scripts, along with some sample voice mail scripts; and tips for successful cold emailing to prospects.

Part III covers *The Introductory Appointment-Setting Script.*

If your calls are made to schedule face-to-face meetings, this part is for you. I walk you through the formula to craft an appointment-setting script, and there are sample scripts that you can adapt and personalize. This section includes sample answers to objections you are sure to hear from prospects, along with scripts to help you qualify prospects, leverage appointments and follow-up with prospects until they finally do schedule that meeting.

If *Your Entire Sale Takes Place Over the Telephone,* Part IV will be especially valuable to you.

First, if you are lucky enough to have prospects calling you, this section will show you how to handle those incoming leads to turn prospects into customers. If you are cold calling, Part IV will show you how to gain your prospect's agreement to have a selling conversation; help you prepare to have that conversation; and equip you to respond to prospect objections, including an entire chapter on this subject. This part contains sample scripts that you can adapt, along with suggestions about questions you can employ to gather information, to gain agreement, and to help close the sale. Because not every sale closes in only one phone call, I have included scripts for following up with prospects until they buy. Last, but certainly not least, Part IV covers scripts to close the sale.

The Performance Model is the framework for ensuring these scripts are effective for you...if you're skeptical about the value of scripting, I suggest you skip ahead to Part V.

Part V explains *The Performance Model* that is the framework for ensuring these scripts are as effective as possible for you. In fact, if you're skeptical about the value of scripting, or not sure that these approaches will work for you, I suggest you skip ahead to Part V to see why I'm so sure they will.

Although many things have changed in telephone sales one thing has remained constant: when you reach a prospect directly you have very little time, perhaps 10-30 seconds, to grab and hold your prospect's attention. This is not the time to be winging it. This is the time to be prepared with the most compelling sales script you can find or create.

And any misstep, the wrong word or inflection while you're on the phone with a prospect, can easily lead to that prospect disengaging. To be successful, you want to be prepared to deliver that persuasive sales script with ease and confidence.

These *Essential Scripts and Strategies to Skyrocket Sales Performance* have all been tried, they've all been tested, and they all work. It is up to you to take the scripts, adapt them to your needs, and internalize them so that they become a part of your process. Reading this book is Step One. If you really want to be successful in sales, take one script at a time and practice it out loud so that it rolls off of your tongue without effort. Then take the next script and do the same thing.

Role-play these scripts with your manager, a colleague, a friend or a coach. Sales trainers are so fond of role-playing because it helps you become automatic in your responses. You want to ensure that when faced with any sales scenario you know exactly what you will say and how you will say it. That only comes with practice.

In addition, think about scripts you are currently using that *are* working for you - and keep them. I recommend that you write everything down. Don't rely on memory - you'll forget. Create a folder in which you keep all your scripts, and whenever you discover a new script that works for you – another compelling answer to a prospect's question, another great way to introduce yourself and your business – add it to your *Script Folder*.

If in the future you are stumped by a prospect objection, that's ok - the first time. Find an answer for that objection by speaking with colleagues or your manager, reading books, taking seminars or working with a coach. Once you've found a good response – or several – memorize it. Add the new script to your *Script Folder* and you will never again be stumped by that objection. There is no dishonor in being stumped by a prospect objection once: there is no good reason to be stumped by the same objection twice.

My intent in writing this *Sales Winner's Handbook* is to give you a jumping-off point: scripts that work. If you have never consciously thought about scripting, this book will be the starting point for your conscious success in sales. If you are

There is no dishonor in being stumped by a prospect objection once: there is no good reason to be stumped by the same objection twice.

already using scripts, use this book to critique your technique, add to your arsenal of sales tools, and bolster your success.

Work with these scripts and adapt them. Do so, and these scripts can make the difference between frustration and failure, or success beyond your wildest dreams. I leave it to you to choose.

To your success!

Wendy Weiss
The Queen of Cold Calling

Part I. Cold Calling in the 21ˢᵗ Century - The New Rules

Is Cold Calling dead? That's what you hear. No one likes making cold calls. No one likes receiving cold calls. The Internet and email have replaced the telephone. Cold calling is old-fashioned. It's not cool. It doesn't work.

Or does it?

In terms of direct marketing, cold calling is actually one of the most targeted, efficient and effective ways to reach potential customers. Nothing beats having a real conversation with a prospect.

Studies back this up.

"Cold calling is second only to referrals as the number one lead generation tactic," is the conclusion of the research report *6 Lead Generation Insights for 2007,* by Mike Schultz and Andrea Meachan Rosal (Publisher and Chief Content Officer, respectively, of *RainToday.com*) with John Doerr (Principal of the Wellesley Hills Group).

And Stefan Tornquist, Research Director of *MarketingSherpa.com*, summarized the state of the industry similarly:

> **"So, yes, that's absolutely an endorsement of good old-fashioned cold calling, especially when it's targeted and appropriate**."
> *MarketingSherpa Business Technology Marketing Presentation 2007*

Cold calling does work, when done right. The issue is that most people do it poorly, which is why it doesn't work for them. This handbook and the scripts it contains will make the difference and be extremely valuable in your efforts to improve lead generation and sales performance.

Stefan Tornquist notes the important point that cold calling must be "targeted and appropriate." Here are some prevalent misconceptions about cold calling:

> ➤ Cold calling is a numbers game: Make 100 dials/day and someone will eventually say, "yes."
> ➤ Cold calling is a numbers game: Go through the "no's" and hang ups until you finally get a "yes."
> ➤ Anyone is a prospect: Open the phone book and start making calls.
> ➤ Practice rebuttals to ensure that you can corner the prospect.
> ➤ Manipulate the prospect into agreeing.
> ➤ ABC: Always Be Closing.

I doubt these tactics were ever truly effective. Ten years ago, maybe – or even five years ago - when it was easier to get people on the telephone, it might have worked to simply keep making calls until someone said "yes." Today one can dial for long periods of time without ever reaching a prospect directly. That is why the "numbers game" idea is a myth.

So is the idea that "anyone is a prospect." Cold calling today is direct, targeted and above all, a communication skill. Those who disparage cold calling are totally missing the point. The bottom line is that no matter where you find a lead, whether from networking or a referral or even if someone contacts you, at some point you will need to speak with that prospect on the telephone, and if you are not able to communicate the value of the product or service that you represent, you won't get the customer.

> **No matter where you find a lead, at some point you will need to speak with that prospect on the telephone, and if you are not able to communicate the value you won't get the customer.**

In today's business environment, however, it is imperative to understand what has changed, what works today and what will simply waste your time - the rules for success with one of the top tactics for generating leads and sales.

Here are the *Cold Calling Rules for the 21st Century*:

1. Have a targeted list.

Before starting a cold calling campaign, create a profile of the ideal prospects you are trying to reach. Out of everyone in the entire world who might buy what you sell, who is most likely to? And who is most likely to buy a lot of what you sell, and keep returning to buy more?

Describe this *Ideal Customer* in specific detail. Consider criteria like:

> ➢ What industry or market?
> ➢ Where are they located?
> ➢ What is the title of the decision-maker?
> ➢ Does this market have challenges or issues that your product or service can solve?
> ➢ If you are calling in the consumer market, what are the demographics of your ideal prospects? Where do they live? Work? Go to school?

These are your *Qualifying Parameters*, the criteria that describe the ideal prospect who is likely to buy, buy a lot, and come back regularly to buy more.

Then only call the leads that fit your *Ideal Customer* profile. If prospects do not meet your parameters, they are not qualified prospects. You will spin your wheels and waste your time trying to reach them, and they will not buy very much or at all.

In business-to-business calls, make sure to only call the highest-level person you believe is the decision-maker. If that person is not the decision-maker, they'll be able to tell you who is. Far too many sales professionals and business owners waste their time calling too low. They do this with the idea that somehow the calls will be easier. They won't. This simply wastes your time and extends your sales cycle. If you are not speaking with a decision-maker, you are not speaking with a qualified prospect. If you are not speaking with a qualified prospect, they will not buy from you.

2. Look for the prospects who are looking for you.

Rule 1 was to create your *Qualifying Parameters* so that you could create a targeted list. Keep these ideal characteristics in mind as you speak with prospects. Remember: you are looking for the **best** prospects, the ones who are most likely to buy, buy again and keep coming back to buy more. The myth is that cold calling is about manipulating prospects into buying things they neither want nor need. The reality is that you are looking for the prospects that are looking for you. So look to qualify your prospects out as well as in. If, during your conversation you realize that a prospect no longer fits your *Qualifying Parameters,* then they are no longer a prospect for you. Let them go.

3. Answer your prospect's question: why should they be interested?

In addition to having a targeted list, your approach must be targeted to the market and the individual that you are calling. It must be relevant. There is no generic approach that will work. Preparation counts, big time.

Ask yourself these questions:

> ➤ What are your prospect's challenges?
> ➤ What is their history?
> ➤ What's happening now?
> ➤ What problems do you solve for your customers?
> ➤ What problems can you potentially solve for your prospects?
> ➤ How do you help your customers?
> ➤ What are the outcomes you/your company/product/ service deliver to customers?

In order to create an approach that will resonate with prospects you must dig deeply to understand them. Do your homework and do the research. They will not tell you; they'll expect you to know. Prospects today are busy; they are bombarded from all sides. If you want to get their attention on a prospecting call you need to have something compelling to say. It must be relevant. Truly understanding your prospects and their situations will help you craft an approach that will enable you to have a productive conversation.

4. Understand the goal of your call.

Many people confuse cold calling with closing a sale. Every sale goes through a cycle, from the introduction to information gathering to offering a solution to closing. Cold calling is <u>not</u> closing a sale. That comes later. Many sales professionals and/ or business owners are making calls to set face-to-face meetings. Others are making calls to schedule web-based demos. Even those whose entire sales process takes place over the telephone must still have some type of introductory conversation with the prospect. The cold call is not the sale – it is the introduction.

This goal frames your entire approach. On your initial contact with a prospect, you are not asking them to buy from you or to agree to let you replace their current vendor. You are only asking to have a productive conversation. This has two advantages. Your prospect feels far less pressure – and you never want a prospect to feel pressure because they will run; and you also feel less pressure, since you don't have to close immediately on the telephone.

One you have that initial comprehensive conversation on the phone or face-to-face, you will know whether or not you are speaking with a truly qualified prospect with a legitimate need that you can satisfy. If you are, you will still need to do all of the relationship building, discovery and offering a solution in order to close the sale.

5. Craft your approach.

While many, many people resist the idea of creating a script, this is simply following through on Rules 3 and 4 above. Bottom line: cold calling is a communication skill. You want your prospects to understand the value that you represent and how it will positively impact them. You want the prospect to be interested and excited by what you have to offer. To achieve that result, you must craft your language.

One thing that has not changed in the 21st century is that you don't have a lot of time to grab and hold a prospect's attention.

It is imperative to be prepared. When you get that prospect on the telephone you must have something compelling to say: this is not the moment to be winging it. If you don't sound interesting or relevant to your prospect they will not want to speak with you. If a prospect says, "I'm not interested" and hangs up, you will not get another chance.

Lead with the value that your provide and use concrete examples to illustrate that value. Make sure to ask for what you want: a meeting, an extended telephone conversation, or scheduling a time for the prospect to see a web-based demo. Over time you will memorize your approach. If you are just starting out, write it down so that you won't have to think about it or worry that you'll forget anything important, and you can simply concentrate on your prospect.

Create *Telephone Theater*. It's not only what you say - it's how you say it. Your voice conveys as much if not more than the words you speak, so take the time to practice your approach out loud. Call your voice mail and record your introductory speech, then listen to how you sound. You want to sound warm, friendly and confident, happy to be speaking with your prospect, and conveying the sense that you have something important to say.

6. Use all the tools that are available.

While it is more difficult to get prospects on the telephone than in the past, the good news is that there are more tools available to you to reach your prospects directly. At one time the only way you could contact a prospect was via their office phone, or perhaps a letter, but today you can also call the prospect's cell phone and/or send an email.

Always try to reach your prospect directly first. It is always better if you can have a conversation. If this is a prospect that you truly want to reach, after several attempts you can leave a voice mail message or send an email. (But see Part II first!)

Remember: As with your telephone script, the rule for a voice mail and/or email is to lead with the value that you provide. That is what will gain your prospect's attention.

7. Have a system.

This is probably the hardest rule for most people to follow. I am constantly surprised by the number of sales professionals and business owners who do not have a good system to track their prospects - or even their customers. In the 21st century, there simply is no excuse for not using some type of contact tracking software.

In addition, set up your "Best Practices" for prospecting. Ask yourself these questions:

> ➤ What are your systems for contacting prospects?
> ➤ How often do you try a prospect before letting them go?
> ➤ What scripts are you using?
> ➤ What scripts are you using for voice mails?
> ➤ What email templates are you using?
> ➤ What is your system to follow up with prospects?
> ➤ What other tools are you using to support your prospecting efforts?

While the answers to these questions are outside the scope of this book, they are very important and will have a great impact on the success of any prospecting campaign.

...you are looking for those prospects who are looking for you.

The environment for cold calling has changed in certain ways, but the bottom line is that cold calling is still one of the top tactics for effective lead generation and sales. It must be targeted, and you must have a compelling, market-focused, value-centered message that will resonate with prospects. Rather than manipulation, cold calling is high-level sorting - you are looking for those prospects who are looking for you. And for cold calling to work best, you must have a system for sorting your prospects. Cold calling is about conversations that lead to conversions.

The days of the "numbers game" and "open the phone book and call" approaches are history. Cold calling is dead: long live cold calling!

Part II.
Gatekeepers and Voice Mail

Every telephone prospecting scenario begins with the attempt to identify the decision-maker and then get that decision-maker on the phone to have a selling conversation. Before reaching your prospect, however, you will usually encounter either human gatekeepers or voice mail, or both.

So how do you successfully get past these barriers to identify the decision-maker and get your prospect on the phone? With the right scripts, of course.

In this chapter you will find scripts for naming the decision-maker and then bypassing gatekeepers to reach your prospect directly. And in the event that despite your best efforts you are unable to reach your prospect directly, I also outline *The Voice Mail Formula* and provide some sample voice mails that you can use and adapt.

You may be calling large companies, or you may be calling smaller companies. The kind of gatekeepers you encounter and your approach to them will differ depending on the size of the company you are calling. Gatekeepers in both small and large companies will ask "What is this in reference to?" – but they actually mean different things by that question. You must know with whom you are speaking, and what they are actually asking you.

There are therefore three kinds of scripts for getting past gatekeepers to decision-makers:

> ➤ *Naming the Decision-Maker*
> ➤ *Calling Large Companies: Secretaries & Assistants*
> ➤ *Calling Small Companies*

We will begin with **Naming the Decision-Maker.** You will use this script for large or small companies when you do not have the name of your prospect.

Chapter 1.
Naming the Decision-Maker

The easiest way to name your prospect is to simply ask the receptionist - or the frontline person who answers the phone.

When you are calling a large company you will probably first encounter a receptionist or switchboard operator. Receptionists in large companies DO NOT screen calls. Their job is to connect calls. They may very well ask you, "What is this in reference to?"

What they really mean by asking that question is that they're not sure with whom they should connect you. You will need to help them out by using what I call the **Broken Record Technique** - you repeat what you just said in different ways, giving more titles as options, until that receptionist or switchboard operator recognizes a title.

On the other hand, if you are calling a small company you will most likely reach someone who actually does screen calls. That's ok. Either way, if you do not know the name of your prospect you'll start out the process in exactly the same way.

To find the person who actually makes the decision, you must ask for a title. You want to find the highest level person that you believe is the decision-maker. If that person is not the decision-maker, they will know who is and can refer you down. And, counter-intuitively, it is much easier to work from the top down than from the bottom up.

One of the biggest mistakes you can make in **Naming the Decision-Maker** is to ask for an activity rather than a title. It's a common mistake: in training and coaching sessions I frequently find that someone will show me their script, and they have been asking for "the person who makes the decision to purchase *(fill in product/service)"* or "the person who purchases *(fill in product/service)."*

This question may get you someone who is involved, most likely as an end user of the product/service, rather than the person who actually makes the decision to buy the product/service. Although it can be very useful to speak with end users to gather qualifying information, ultimately you must reach the person who makes the decision.

Even worse, when calling small companies the request for "the person who makes the decision to purchase *(fill in product/service)"* or "the person who purchases *(fill in product/service)"* will frequently elicit responses such as "We're all covered" or "We're not interested," or "Send an email and if we're interested we'll call you back." This question can be the kiss of death for your call, so don't ask it!

Script for Naming the Decision-Maker

You:

"Before you connect me (P A U S E), I need to reach…" *(give title)* "Who is that please?"

*The key word here is: "**before**." You say, "Before you connect me" and then you pause because you want the receptionist to hear the word "before" and give you a name before she puts you through.*

The key word here is: "before."

Receptionist:

"What is this in reference to?"

This "What is this in reference to?" is different than later on when the decision-maker's secretary or assistant says it. At this point the receptionist really means "I do not understand what you want, I don't know who to connect you with."

You:

*Use the **Broken Record Technique** - repeat what you just said but elaborate a little.*

"I need to reach whoever is over all in charge of *(department where decision is made).* I don't know if that would be your Director of *(title)* or your Vice President of *(title)* or your Manager of *(title).* Who would handle that and what is the correct title?

*If you keep using the **Broken Record Technique** and throwing out titles, eventually the receptionist will latch onto one and give you a name.*

If a company has a policy that the switchboard will not give out names, you can ask to be connected with the department where the decision is likely to be made. When you reach the receptionist or the frontline person who answers the phone in that area, start over with the script: "Before you connect me (P A U S E)…"

If you are calling a small company it is more than likely that the decision-maker you want to reach is the Owner, President, CEO or some similar title. You probably will want to speak with the person who runs the company. In a small company there may be many people involved in the decision, but most of the time the ultimate decision-maker is going to be the person who runs the company. If you start there you will eliminate the "I have to ask my boss" syndrome that stalls so many sales.

This is the script for **Naming the Decision-Maker** when you call small companies:

You:

"Before you connect me *(P A U S E)*, I need to reach the company owner. Who is that please?

Gatekeeper:

"What is this in reference to?"

Treat this "What is this in reference to?" as a receptionist question. You are being asked for information: help out.

You:

*Use the **Broken Record Technique** - repeat what you just said but elaborate a little.*

"I need to reach whoever is over all in charge of the company. I don't know if that would be your President or your CEO or the owner of the company. Who would that be and what is the correct title?

*If you keep using the **Broken Record Technique** and throwing out titles, eventually the gatekeeper will latch onto one and give you a name.*

Gatekeeper:

That's *(prospect's name)*.

When you are calling small companies, it's at this point that the Gatekeeper might start asking additional questions. These will be *Screening Questions,* which we will cover in Chapter 2.

Six More Ways to Name Your Prospect

If you are having a difficult time putting a name on the correct prospect, here are some additional easy ways to discover with whom you should be speaking. The key script that you need to know is:

> "I'm wondering if you can help me."

These are magical words. People love to help, and if you ask, most people will be very responsive to your request. Employ these magic words as often as you can in your hunt for your prospect.

"I'm wondering if you can help me."

1. Check the prospect **company's web site**. This is the easiest way to find your prospect's name. Thanks to the Internet, many companies today list executive and/or senior management on their web sites, sometimes with organizational charts.

2. **Call the Chief Executive Officer.** The theory here is that Executive Assistants know everything. Call the CEO's office and ask the Executive Assistant for some help, with "I'm wondering if you can help me." Tell the Executive Assistant exactly what you need and more than likely you will be pointed in the right direction.

3. Randomly **change the general switchboard number extensions**. If the switchboard number is 5000, call 5001, 5002... until you reach a human being. It won't be the right human being, but that's ok. Once you reach a human being, ask that person to help you: "I'm wondering if you can help me." Ask, "Do you have a company directory?

Could you look that up for me, please?" When asked this way, most people are very happy to help. Be sure to thank this person profusely.

4. The **made-up name**. Sometimes companies will not give out information unless you have a name. In this case, make up a name and then ask for that person. The switchboard operator will tell you there is no one there by that name. You then say, "Oh, *(made up name)* used to be the *(title)*. Who has taken over there?" Many times this will work to get you the right name.

5. **Ask a sales person**. Call the sales department and speak with a sales person. Say, "I'm wondering if you can help me." Sales people will understand your situation and if they can, they will help you. Tell the sales person exactly who you are trying to reach, and don't forget the *Broken Record Technique*: use variations on titles to help them help you. If they do not know the correct name of the Decision-Maker, ask, "Do you have a directory handy? Could you look that up for me, please?" Be sure to thank this person profusely for their help.

6. **Ask Customer Service**. Customer Service is there to help. Call them and ask: "I'm wondering if you can help me." Many times Customer Service can give you the information you require. Again, if the Customer Service representative does not know the correct name ask, "Do you have a directory handy? Could you look that up for me, please?" Be sure to thank this person profusely for their help.

Chapter 2. Gatekeepers: Secretaries and Assistants

Gatekeepers in Large Companies: Secretaries and Assistants

Once you have named the decision-maker, the next human being you might encounter on your path to speaking directly with your prospect is that person's secretary or assistant. Secretaries and/or assistants *do* screen calls. That is part of their job.

Another part of their job is to put important calls through - including your call. Your job is to either get the decision-maker on the phone, or find out when you can reach the decision-maker directly and call back then.

Your posture needs to be that of a peer of the decision-maker. Your tone should be confident and firm and always polite. You control the conversation by asking questions or giving direction as you will see in the following script:

Script for Secretaries and Assistants

You:

Ask for your Prospect by first and last name.

"*(Prospect's name)*, please."

Secretary/Assistant:

"Who's calling?"

You:

"This is *(your name)*. Is she available?"

Secretary/Assistant:

"Where are you calling from?"

You:

"*(Company name)*. Is she available?"

Note: If your company name says exactly what you do – for example, ABC Printing Company – then shorten the name to simply ABC.

Secretary/Assistant:

"What is this in reference to?"

You:

"Please tell *(prospect's name)* that *(your name)* from *(your company)* is on the line."

If the Secretary/Assistant says your prospect is unavailable...

"He's on the phone."

"She's away from her desk."

"He's in a meeting."

"She's out of the office."

"He's not available."

...You must ask targeted questions:

"When will he be finished with that call?"

"When will she return?"

"What time do you expect him to be back?"

"How late will she be in this afternoon?"

"When is the best time to reach him?"

Additional responses to "What is this in reference to?"

Secretary/Assistant:

"What is this in reference to?"

You:

"It's rather complex and it's something I need to discuss with *(prospect's name)*. Is she available?"

Your next response depends on the secretary. If the secretary/ assistant tells you the decision-maker is not available, use targeted questions such as those above to find out when you can call back. On the other hand, the secretary/assistant may say:

Secretary/Assistant:

"I need more information. (I need to tell him what this call is about.)"

You:

"Please tell *(prospect's name)* that *(your name)* from *(your company)* is on the line. That should be fine."

OR

Secretary/Assistant:

"Will she know what this is in reference to?"

You:

"She may not. Please tell *(prospect's name)* that *(your name)* from *(your company)* is on the line."

If you've sent information, an email or a letter in advance:

Secretary/Assistant:

"What is this in reference to?"

You:

"We've had correspondence. Please tell *(prospect's name)* that *(your name)* from *(your company)* is on the line."

These scripts will enable you to quickly reach prospects that are available, and if your prospects are not available, quickly find out when you might be able to reach them directly.

Remember, however: these scripts are not magic. Not everyone will be available when you call, so if you are not able to reach any particular prospect, gather as much information as you can from any Gatekeepers to ascertain when you might be able to reach your prospect; mark that prospect for another phone call on a day and time that they might be available; then move on and call the next prospect.

...if you are not able to reach any particular prospect, gather as much information as you can from any Gatekeepers...

If the Secretary/ Assistant Wants to Take a Message

Never leave a message with a human being. If you are going to leave a message, leave it on voice mail. If you leave a message on voice mail, you know that your prospect will hear your message *exactly* as you want it to be heard. If you leave your message with a human being you have no control of how the message actually comes out.

Sometimes a secretary/assistant may be very insistent about taking a message. If that happens use this script:

You:

> "I'm heading into a meeting and she won't be able to reach me. I'll give her a buzz later. When is the best time to check back?"

Secretary/Assistant:

> "When you call back you'll still have to tell me what it's in reference to..."

You:

> "I'll be happy to give you whatever information you need when I check back. I'm not going to leave a message

right now. Thank you."

Then when you call back, start all over with:

You:

"*(Prospect's name)*, please."

Calling Small Companies Where One Person May Be Both The Receptionist And The Secretary/Assistant

When calling small companies you will often only encounter one level of screening: there will only be one front line person, who plays both roles of Receptionist and Secretary.

If you already know your prospect's name, simply proceed with the *Script for Secretaries and Assistants* on the previous pages.

If you need to first Name The Decision-Maker, however, you will use a combination of the *Script for Naming the Decision-Maker* and the *Script for Secretaries and Assistants*.

You:

"Before you connect me *(P A U S E)*, I need to reach the company owner. Who is that please?"

Gatekeeper:

"What is this in reference to?"

Treat this "What is this in reference to?" as a receptionist question. You are being asked for information: help out.

You:

*Use the **Broken Record Technique** - repeat what you just said but elaborate a little.*

"I need to reach whoever is over all in charge of the

company. I don't know if that would be your President or your CEO or the owner of the company. Who would that be and what is the correct title?

*If you keep using the **Broken Record Technique** and throwing out titles, eventually the gatekeeper will latch onto one and give you a name.*

Gatekeeper:

That's *(prospect's name)*, but what is this in reference to?

At this point, you know that this is one person who doubles as Receptionist and Secretary. Receptionists who are only receptionists do not screen. If the receptionist gives you a name and then asks, "What is this in reference to?" you must now use your Secretary/Assistant screening techniques.

You:

"Please tell *(prospect's name)* that *(your name)* from *(your company)* is on the line."

Chapter 3. Voice Mail

Once you have named your prospect, the next issue is to actually get that prospect on the telephone. Today many, many calls go to voice mail without ever reaching a human being.

While many prospectors leave messages with the hope that the prospect will call back, very few prospects do actually return phone calls. Coupled with that is the reality that you are always better off being able to have a conversation with your prospect.

A conversation makes that human being to human being connection. You are able to hear your prospect, what they are saying and how they are saying it. You can respond to your prospect's questions. You can accomplish so much more if you can only speak with your prospect directly. So how do you align these two realities - that you need to actually speak with your prospect and that so many calls go directly to voice mail?

The answer is to bypass voice mail by being a detective and actively seeking out your prospect. Here are:

12 Strategies to Bypass Voice Mail

1. **Ask the gatekeeper:** "When is the best time to reach *(prospect's name)?*" Call back then.

2. **Vary your calling times.** If you are only reaching voice mail you have no way of ascertaining when your prospect will be available. If you always make your calls at the same time of day, vary your routine. Call at different times throughout the day and throughout the week.

3. **Ask for alternate phone numbers for your prospect.** Ten years ago prospects generally only had one office line. Today there are a myriad of ways to reach prospects: cell phones, home office phones. Your prospect might have another office location and of course, there is always email. Make sure that you get all of your prospect's contact information.

4. **Call prospects outside of business hours.** High level decision-makers are frequently in their offices at times that their secretaries or assistants are not and often during those times they answer their own phones. Calling before 9:00 a.m. and after 5:00 p.m. can often help you bypass voice mail and reach your prospect directly. Always ask gatekeepers for your prospects' direct line. This way you will be able to reach your prospect early or after business hours.

5. **Call prospects during lunch.** When you are calling high-level decision-makers lunchtime is the second best time to call. If your prospect does not have a lunch meeting scheduled, they could very well be at their desk having a working lunch. During these times gatekeepers are frequently not there and the prospect might actually be answering their own phone.

6. If possible, **block your phone number.** Depending on the state in which you live and of course, your work situation, you may be able to block your phone number from showing up on a prospect's caller ID. If you can block your number this will allow you to call a prospect more frequently as your prospect will not know it is you calling.

7. If you cannot block your line, **dial *67** before you dial your prospect's number. This strategy will allow you to block the line for that call. This will enable you to call a prospect more frequently as your prospect will not know it is you calling.

8. **Call the extension with one number up or down from your prospect's number.** The idea here is that you might reach someone who sits near or has an office near your prospect. Ask: "When is the best time to reach *(prospect's name)*?" "What time does *(prospect's name)* come in?" "What time does *(prospect's name)* take lunch?" "How late is *(prospect's name)* usually in?" Be a detective, gather information and call back when you think you might be able to reach that prospect directly.

9. **Dial 0 for help.** Usually at the end of an outgoing message is a statement like, "If you need additional or immediate help dial…" or "To reach someone else in the company dial…" Take advantage of this. You might have to leave a message so that the system will let you move onto the next step. If you don't want to leave an actual message you can simply say, "OK" which will be recorded and then allow you to move on. As in #5, ask the person that you reach for help.

10. **Send your prospect an e-mail and attach a "read receipt."** Keep your e-mail open. When you receive the read receipt back, try calling your prospect. That prospect could very well be at their desk or holding their Blackberry in their hand.

11. **Call the wrong number.** Yes, deliberately call a wrong

number within your target company. That's right, any
wrong number so long as it's within the company. You
will of course, reach the wrong person. That's ok. When
you reach the wrong person, ask them to transfer you
to the number you wish to reach. Your call will now look
like it's coming from someone internally. If the prospect
is screening their calls and not picking up calls
that come from outside lines, they may very well answer
the phone thinking it's someone within the company.

12. As a last resort, if you absolutely must reach a particular
prospect, **ask if that prospect can be paged.**

Leaving Messages

There are certain circumstances where you may decide to leave a voice mail message. You've hunted for your prospect and have simply not been able to reach that person directly. If this is a particularly important prospect or if there is a specific time frame in which you have to reach your prospect, you may feel that you'd be better off leaving a voice mail message.

If that is the case, be strategic and set up the best possible situation to increase the likelihood that your prospect will call you back. You will want to use *The Voice Mail Formula.* Here's an outline of that, after which you will find some sample *Voice Mail Scripts* that you can adapt to your own use.

The Voice Mail Formula

> ➤ **Say your name and telephone number at least twice**, slowly, once at the beginning of the message, once at the end. Your prospect will not call you back if they do not have your phone number. Say your name and phone number at the speed you would if dictating to someone who is going to write it down. Your prospect will interpret this slow dictation as a prompt to write, and will pick up a pen and begin to write. Make sure to say your number again slowly at the end of the message. This way if your prospect missed the number the first time, they won't have to go back to the beginning of the message. Make it easy for your prospect to call you back.

Make it easy for your prospect to call you back.

> ➤ **Spell your name**. If your name is at all difficult, spell it. Spell it slowly the same way you did with your phone number. You want your prospect to be able to write your name down correctly.

> ➤ **Speak slowly and distinctly**. If your prospect does not understand you, they will not call you back, so make sure

that you speak clearly.

> **Focus your message on the value, benefits and outcomes** that you, your products/services or company can deliver to customers. This is the heart of your message. The tips above ensure that your prospect will be able to call you back. Focusing on the value will ensure that your prospect will _want_ to call you back.

> **Tell a _Success Story_.** Tell your prospect about similar companies with whom you have worked and how you were able to help them. Keep this short: 3-4 sentences should be enough. (For more on _Success Stories_ see _Part III, Chapter 2._)

> The likelihood is minimal that a prospect will call you back after only one message. You must therefore, **create a series (3-8) of differing voice mail messages**. You will want to tell different _Success Stories_ or focus on a different value or outcome in each message, so that you are saying something new each time that you call. **Leave one message every 3-5 business days.** This repetition increases the likelihood that your prospect may call you back. If one message does not resonate, perhaps the next will. The number of messages that you leave is contingent on the importance of the prospect you are trying to reach. As a standard best practice you might leave 4 voice mails before moving on. If, on the other hand, you feel that it is vitally important to reach this particular prospect, then leave more messages.

> If you have left your series of messages and have not received a return call, in your last voice mail message you must be sure to tell your prospect that **you will not be calling again**. Make sure that you keep an even, pleasant tone and use neutral words - nothing that could be interpreted as angry or annoyed. Let your prospect know that you know that they are busy. Tell them you're assuming that it is not a good time for them to have the discussion, and so you will not be calling again for a

while. Specify a time frame: this quarter, in six months, this year... Sometimes the statement that you won't be calling can make an interested (but extremely busy) prospect pick up the telephone and call you back.

➤ Make sure that you keep track of the voice mail messages you leave. Many sales representatives simply write, "left message" in their notes. You want to be able to remember which message you left so that you know which message to leave next, and also so that you know which messages get good responses. If your CRM or prospecting software does this automatically, that's great. Most do not, however, so write it down in your notes. (See the *Sales Resource Guide* for recommendations for prospecting software and CRM.)

Generic scripts do not work. The more specific that you are about your credentials, history and outcomes for customers, the more success you will have.

Sample Voice Mail Messages

Please note: These are samples – templates - only. You must use your own company credentials, statistics, customers and *Success Stories.*

Generic scripts do not work. The more specific that you are about your credentials, history and outcomes for customers, the more success you will have.

Please also read Parts II and III on Scripting to help you craft your voice mail messages.

Sample Voice Mail Sequence for a Point of Sale System

Voice Mail #1

Hello *(prospect name)*.

This is *(your name)*. I'm with XYZ Associates. *(Your phone number)*.

We're experts in retail point of sale systems that increase *(niche)* stores' sales and profitability.

The bottom line is: In this recession we're helping clients cut their overhead, cut unnecessary sales and discounts, and turn nonselling merchandise into revenue.

For example, ABC Store saw an increase of almost 30% using our system.

I'd like to introduce myself and XYZ Associates personally, learn about your store and see if we might be able to help. Please call me.

Again this is *(your name)* from XYZ Associates. Our phone number is *(your phone number)*.

Voice Mail #2

Hello *(prospect name)*.

This is *(your name)*. I'm with XYZ Associates. *(Your phone number)*.

We're experts in retail point of sale systems that increase *(niche)* stores' sales and profitability.

We've been supporting retailers for *(number of)* years and we work with over *(number of)* clients in nearly *(number of)* retail locations throughout the United States.

For example: DEF Stores saw an increase in sales of (*percentage*) after using our system.

I'd like to introduce myself and XYZ Associates personally, learn about your store and see if we might be able to help. Please call me.

Again this is (*your name*) from XYZ Associates. Our phone number is (*your phone number*).

Voice Mail #3

Hello (*prospect name*).

This is (*your name*). I'm with XYZ Associates. (*Your phone number*).

We're experts in retail point of sale systems that help store owners track and maintain inventory and increase customer loyalty.

For example HIJ Store was losing customers to the competition because they were having a hard time tracking inventory. They simply didn't always know what they had in the store or when they needed to reorder. Customers would come in and if HIJ didn't have what they needed, the customer would go elsewhere.

Once they installed our system that never happened again. They never lost another customer due to not having the inventory.

I'd like to introduce myself and XYZ Associates personally, learn about your store and see if we might be able to help. Please call me.

Again this is (*your name*) from XYZ Associates. Our phone number is (*your phone number*).

Voice Mail #4

Hello *(prospect name)*.

This is *(your name)*. I'm with XYZ Associates. *(Your phone number)*.

We're experts in retail point of sale systems that help store owners increase sales and profitability.

I've called you a few times wanting to introduce myself and XYZ Associates personally. I know that you are very busy, and because I haven't heard back from you I'm assuming this is not a good time for us to have a conversation. I don't want to make a pest of myself and so I will not be calling again. I'll touch base in six months or so.

If you've been meaning to call back and simply haven't had the chance, I would love to share with you how we've helped other store owners in the area. Please call me.

Again this is *(your name)* from XYZ Associates. Our phone number is *(your phone number)*.

Sample Voice Mail Sequence for a Credit Card Processing Company

Voice Mail #1

Hello *(prospect name)*.

My name is *(your name)*. My phone number is *(your phone number)*.

I'm a Consultant with XYZ Company. The security of customer information is a huge issue today and we are known for helping local restaurants control and maintain the security of their operations.

We've been in business since (*date*) and work with *Restaurant A, Restaurant B, Restaurant C* right in the neighborhood.

I'd like to share with you how we've been able to help other restaurant owners in the area sleep easier at night knowing that their customer data will not be compromised. Please call me.

Again this is (*your name*) from XYZ Company. Our phone number is (*your phone number*).

Voice Mail #2

Hello (*prospect name*).

My name is (*your name*). My phone number is (*your phone number*).

I'm a Consultant with XYZ Company. Given our current economy every restaurant owner that I know is really watching their bottom line and we are known for helping local restaurant owners manage and control their expenses.

We've been in business since (*date*) and work with *Restaurant A, Restaurant B, Restaurant C* right in the neighborhood.

I'd like to share with you how we've been able to help other restaurant owners in the area control their operating expenses. Please call me.

Again this is (*your name*) from XYZ Company. Our phone number is (*your phone number*).

Voice Mail #3

Hello (*prospect name*).

My name is (*your name*). My phone number is (*your phone number*).

I'm a Consultant with XYZ Company and we stand up for the little guy. We are known for helping local restaurant owners have the same clout and competitive edge in the marketplace as the TV chefs with big restaurants.

We've been in business since *(date)* and work with *Restaurant A, Restaurant B, Restaurant C* right in the neighborhood.

I'd like to share with you how we've been able to help other restaurant owners in the area gain the competitive edge in the market. Please call me.

Again this is *(your name)* from XYZ Company. Our phone number is *(your phone number)*.

Voice Mail #4

Hello *(prospect name).*

My name is *(your name).* My phone number is *(your phone number).*

I'm a Consultant with XYZ Company and we work with local restaurant owners to help them control and manage their operating expenses and ensure their customer data is secure.

I've called you a few times wanting to introduce myself and XYZ Company personally. I know that you are very busy and because I have not heard back from you I'm assuming this is not a good time for us to have a conversation. I don't want to make a pest of myself and so I will not be calling again. I'll touch base in six months or so.

If you've been meaning to call back and simply haven't had the chance, I would love to share with you how we've helped other restaurant owners in the area. Please call me.

Again this is *(your name)* from XYZ Company. Our phone number is (your phone number).

Chapter 4. Email Strategies

Ten Email Strategies to Reach Decision-Makers

In the maze of Corporate America it can be very difficult to get a decision-maker on the telephone. While the title of this book refers to *"Essential Scripts,"* the reality is that sometimes the best way to reach a prospect is via email. If a gatekeeper (especially a secretary or assistant) tells you that the best way to reach a particular prospect is by email, by all means send one. Here are some strategies to maximize your email response:

> **Create an attention-grabbing subject line**. If your prospect does not open your email - or worse still, deletes your email - you are nowhere. Be sure that you have an attention-grabbing subject line. Go to the nearest news stand and look at magazine headlines: use these headlines as a model. Your topic is, of course, different.

> **Subject lines that use the prospect's name and/or subject lines that ask questions** frequently work well. If you have a referral, put that referral's name in the subject line: for example, "Jane Jones recommended that I contact you." If your prospect does not read your e-mail, your sales process stops.

> **Your subject line should be no more than 50 characters.** That's all that will show in your prospect's preview pane. To test what your prospect will see, send the email to yourself. While everyone's inbox is configured differently, doing this will give you an idea of what your prospect will see.

> Subject lines that are in all capital letters or that have exclamation marks will almost certainly get caught in spam filters: **use upper and lower case letters and avoid exclamation marks.**

- ➤ **Keep your email short and to the point**, no more than one screen in length. Remember that your prospect may be reading on their desktop or they may be reading on a Blackberry or another small-screen, handheld device.

- ➤ Just like a voice mail message, **your email must focus on a benefit or result** that you/your company/your product or service can achieve for customers.

- ➤ **Lead with the most important information and/or biggest benefit.** Why? Because you only have one opportunity to make a first impression. That lead-in is what will keep your prospect reading. Make sure that your lead-in is something that your prospect cares about.

- ➤ Be sure that **your message includes a *call to action***. What action do you want your prospect to take? If you want a phone call, you must say, "Please call me." Don't expect that your prospect will guess. It's your job to ask.

- ➤ **No attachments.** Remember that your prospect may be reading on their desktop or they may be reading on their Blackberry or another handheld device. Attachments also frequently get caught in spam filters, which means that your email may not be delivered at all. In addition, attachments sometimes contain computer viruses, so a cautious email recipient will not open an email from a stranger that has an attachment.

- ➤ **No HTML or fancy graphics**. Remember that your prospect may be reading on their desktop or they may be reading on their Blackberry or other handheld device. In addition, some graphics can get caught in spam filters, which means that your email may not be delivered at all.

Use these strategies to script your e-mails so as to increase the chances of beginning a conversation with your prospect.

Part III. The Introductory Appointment-Setting Script

Many sales professionals and business owners make calls to set up face-to-face appointments with prospects. When calling to schedule appointments, it is imperative to be prepared in advance. These days it is far more difficult to get prospects on the telephone than ever before. When you do get your prospect on the line you really need something compelling to say.

Your *Appointment-Setting Script* is different from the script that you would use if your entire sales process takes place over the telephone. This is one of the most common mistakes I have observed in training and coaching sessions over the years, and it's one of the biggest, too: sales representatives trying to convince prospects that their product/service is better than the competition's – in their first, introductory call. They use this as the reason a prospect should meet.

This approach usually backfires, however, because you are essentially asking your prospect to make an immediate buying decision. If you are selling a high ticket product/service that has a long sales cycle, that buying decision is not going to happen in one phone call. To be effective, you must respect the process. Your cold call is the introduction that gets you the appointment, and the appointment is your opportunity to introduce yourself personally, and your company and product/service in more detail. That is it.

If your prospect feels from your approach or your questions that you are asking them to make a buying decision in this first introductory call, they will push back. Your approach can actually create prospect resistance, so be sure to focus on the idea that you simply want to introduce yourself. If you do so, the entire prospecting process changes: you will feel less pressure because you don't have to close in one call, and your prospect won't feel pushed into a corner and forced to make a decision (which at this stage is likely to work against you).

This approach actually pre-empts many objections that you might hear, such as the very common response:

"I already have a vendor."

If you approach your prospect with the idea that you simply want to introduce yourself, the fact that the prospect "already has a vendor" is actually totally irrelevant. Although it is certainly true that your long term goal is to turn the prospect into a customer, the goal of your first phone call is to set up an introductory meeting. Your truthful response can easily be:

"I understand that you have a vendor. Right now I'd simply like to introduce myself...

You side-step the issue entirely. Remember: if you get the appointment, you will have time to answer this objection in detail. (You'll find more on answering objections later, in *Chapter 4 and in Part IV, Chapter 5.*)

So how do you successfully set up face-to-face appointments when you get a prospect on the phone? By using **The Appointment-Setting Script Formula.** This contains all of the elements that you need in an appointment-setting script in order to grab and hold your prospect's attention and gain their commitment to meeting with you.

First, I will outline *The Script Formula* and describe its logic, and then you'll find some sample *Appointment-Setting Scripts* that you can adapt to your own use.

You also will find some important tips about *Pre-empting Prospect Objections*, using *Success Stories* to make your point and the formula for *Responding to Prospect Objections*.

Finally, you'll get some crucial guidance on further *Qualifying Your Prospects*, on *Following Up* on appointment-setting, and *Leveraging Your Appointments*.

Let's start with Appointment-Setting. This Script Formula has four key features:

➢ *The Personal & Company Introduction*
➢ *Your/Your Company's Credentials*
➢ *The Success Story (or Stories)*
➢ *The Appointment-Setting Mantra*

Chapter 1. The Appointment-Setting Script Formula

> **Introduce yourself.**

Hello, *(prospect name)*. My name is *(your name)*. I'm with *(company name)*.

> **One sentence sound bite describing your company and the product/services you offer.**

We are known for *(fill in with the outcome/benefit/results/ value that you/your company/product/service bring to customers)*.

> **Position yourself as the expert - mention Credentials.**

We've been in business for/since (*number of years/date*) and work with (*name 2-3 customers*).

> ➤ **Articulate benefits - tell a *Success Story.***

(*A success story is a true story about a customer, their issue/ challenge and how you/your company/product/service were able to help. This should be a maximum of 2-4 sentences.*)

> ➤ **Ask for the *Appointment.***

I'd like to introduce myself and (*company name*). I need 10-15 minutes, whenever is good for you. Can we carve out a few minutes next week or is the week after better?"

When asking for the appointment, always use **The Appointment-Setting Mantra:**

I'd like to introduce myself and (*company name*). I need 10-15 minutes, whenever is good for you. Can we carve out a few minutes next week or is the week after better?"

This is a 'mantra' because you will keep repeating it.

You'll notice that *The Appointment-Setting Mantra* uses the *Alternate Choice* or *Assuming the Sale Close*: "Can we carve out a few minutes *next week* or is the *week after* better?" You are offering (limited) alternatives and allowing your prospect to choose. Because the prospect is choosing, they feel in control. Because you are the one proposing the set of alternatives, you are really the one in control.

The Appointment-Setting Mantra changes the conversation from *if* a prospect will meet with you to *when* the prospect will meet with you. The conversation then becomes a negotiation.

Note: In this script for the Appointment-Setting Mantra we asked for 10 minutes. You can ask for more time. What is important is that you: 1) ask for the meeting, and 2) put boundaries on the time frame so that your prospects know that you are respectful of their time.

The most important part of the *Script Formula* is *The Appointment-Setting Mantra.* One of the biggest reasons that prospectors are unable to schedule appointments with prospects is that they do not ask – or do not ask more than once. Be sure that you ask the prospect to meet with you. If you hear an objection, respond to it and ask again for the meeting. You will find scripts and formulas for responding to appointment-setting objections, in detail, in *Chapter 4.*

> **One of the biggest reasons that prospectors are unable to schedule appointments with prospects is that they do not ask - or do not ask more than once.**

Chapter 2. Success Stories

A *Success Story* is an edited-down case study. It's a true story about a customer, their issue/challenge, and how you/your company/product/service were able to help. This should be brief and to the point, no more than 2-4 sentences long.

Human beings are story tellers. We like to hear stories: we like to tell stories. Using a *Success Story* in your scripts can be very, very powerful. You can use *Success Stories* in your appointment-setting script, in the script you use if your entire sale takes place over the telephone, and in your face-to-face meetings with prospects.

Success Stories allow you to illustrate benefits without having to say, "And the benefit to you, Ms. Prospect, is…" When you tell a story about how you/your company/product/service were able to help overcome another customer's challenges, your new prospect will instinctively understand that you'll be able to help them in a similar way.

Success Stories in a telephone prospecting script act as third party endorsements – a recommendation of your company/product/service by a neutral third party. An example: If a restaurant puts a big sign in their window say, "We're the best restaurant in town," everyone knows that the restaurant bought and paid for the sign and put it up in their window. This is advertising.

A restaurant review in your local paper that says "It's the best restaurant in town" would be a third party endorsement. The reviewer would be acting as a neutral party endorsing the restaurant. Another example would be if a friend encourages you make a reservation because "It's the best restaurant in town." This is also a third party endorsement, an endorsement from someone who has nothing at stake.

People perceive third party endorsements as being far more credible than advertising, especially if they think the recommendation comes from a neutral and knowledgeable source. When you tell a *Success Story* it acts as a third party endorsement. Even though you are the one telling the story, the *Success Story* is actually about someone else - your customer, the neutral third party. You are simply stating the facts.

A note here: **Success Stories must be true**. Although I am using the word "story," these examples cannot be fiction. You must always be honest with prospects. If you are not, it will come back to hurt you.

Here is the formula for a *Success Story*:

> ➢ *The Customer's Problem*
> ➢ *What You/Your Company/Product/Service Did*
> ➢ *How the Customer was Helped*

Let's say that you're a printer. A *Success Story* might be something like:

"XYZ Company sent us the file for the job that needed to be printed. They were in a panic because there was a problem with the file and they were on a tight deadline. Because of our experience we were able to quickly solve the problem and open the file. We got the job printed before their deadline."

Or let's say you're a commercial real estate broker. A *Success Story* might be along these lines:

"We recently worked with ABC Law Firm. They needed more space and less expensive space and thought they were going to have to move their offices. Instead we helped them find additional space in their building and helped them renegotiate their lease so that they actually saved money and avoided any business disruption."

Success Stories are always focused on the customer, their challenges and how you were able to help. Occasionally in training and coaching sessions someone will show me their script and I'll find that the *Success Story* is something like this:

Success Stories are always focused on the customer, their challenges and how you were able to help.

"ABC Company bought 100 units of our new Ultra-Widget. They were so happy that they came back to us and bought 500 more."

This is <u>not</u> a *Success Story*. While it might be an illustration of a personal success (you sold more units), it is not a *Success Story* that will resonate with a prospect. What's the difference? The first two examples are all about the customer. The last example is about the sales representative. Don't make this mistake.

Chapter 3. Sample Introductory Appointment-Setting Scripts

Please note: These are samples – templates - only. You must use your own company credentials, statistics, customers and *Success Stories.*

Generic scripts do not work. The more specific that you are about your credentials, history and outcomes for customers, the more success you will have.

Appointment-Setting Script for Technology Company

Hello, (*prospect name*).

My name is (*your name*) and I'm with (*company name*). Our expertise is keeping systems running and secure from data theft, attacks, systems failure...

We've been in business for 20 years, and we work with (*Company A, Company B and Company C*)...

The bottom line is... businesses are losing millions of dollars rebuilding damaged resources. They think they're protected, and then it turns out that they're not. Quite a number of our customers have come to us, unfortunately, after they've lost dollars, employee productivity and sometimes they've lost customers.

For example: *XYZ Company* came to us recently concerned that their data might not be as secure as it needed to be. Luckily they came to us before they had any major problems. We worked with them to minimize any problems that had occurred and to ensure that their data would be secure from here on.

We'd like to introduce ourselves personally. We need 15-20

minutes, whenever is good for you. Can we carve out a few minutes next week or is the week after better?

Appointment-Setting Script for Commercial Real Estate

Hello, (*prospect's name*). My name is (*your name*) I'm with (*company name*).

I'm a commercial real estate consultant and my expertise is helping law practices save money on office space.

We've been in business since (*year*) and we work with (*Law Firm A, Law Firm B and Law Firm C*)...

We recently worked with *ABC Law Firm*. They needed more space and less expensive space and so thought they were going to have to move their offices. Instead we helped them find additional space in their building and helped them renegotiate their lease so that they actually saved money on their new lease.

I'd like to introduce myself and (*company name*) personally. I need 10-15 minutes, whenever is good for you. Can we carve out a few minutes next week or is the week after better?

Chapter 4. Answering Objections

Pre-empting Prospect Objections

Far too many sales professionals hear prospect objections as personal rejection. Because of this, many sales professionals are terrified of prospect objections. Rather than being something scary, however, the truth is that an objection from your prospect is important information. You are learning about your prospect, how that prospect thinks and feels and what is important to them. Listen carefully.

That said, however, you do not necessarily have to hear every prospect objection. There are some that you can and should eliminate at the very start of your sales process. This is called "preempting objections."

Many prospect objections occur because the prospector has not done their homework. Before you ever call or meet with a prospect you want to make sure that your prospect is indeed a viable prospect - that the prospect matches your 'ideal customer profile.'

The 'ideal customer profile' is the profile of the type of customer that is most likely to buy what you're selling, buy a lot of it and then come back and buy more. Far too many sales professionals spend their time calling on prospects who do not match their 'ideal customer profile.' This creates objections.

Last week I received an email from someone who had just had a very difficult conversation with a prospect. She felt that her prospect was extremely rude to her and she was quite upset about the conversation. She finished her email to me saying, "And he wasn't even a very good prospect. He probably wouldn't even buy very much!"

I emailed back, "Why were you calling him in the first place?" When you call on a prospect that is not a good match for your offering you are making things harder for yourself. That type of prospect does not need or want what you have to offer - of course there are objections!

Sales professionals can first begin to eliminate objections by making sure they are spending their time only speaking with highly qualified prospects.

Once you begin your conversation with your prospect, the best way to handle prospect objections is to pre-empt them: to address them before the prospect ever brings them up.

If there are common objections that you frequently hear you are much better off addressing those up front in your initial script. This is an incredibly powerful way to minimize the number of objections your prospect might raise.

A very frequent objection prospectors hear is: "It's too expensive" - as in "I've heard about your company and you're too expensive." If you hear this frequently, you can eliminate the power of this objection by addressing it first. If indeed your product/service is more expensive than the competition's, there is probably a reason for that additional cost. What is the reason? Is it that your company uses superior quality products in manufacturing? Does your company offer a special level of service above and beyond what the competition offers?

Identify the reason that your product/service is more expensive than your competitors. Then bring it up yourself as a **value**, not a cost, for your prospect. An example:

> "Our product/service is certainly not the cheapest. That's because we use superior quality materials and offer 24/7 service. None of our competitors can say that."

Another example: Let's say that your company has been having service issues and that these problems are widely known. You're certain that your prospect knows about the issues and will see them as a negative. If the issues have been corrected or are in the process of being corrected you should bring this up first:

"While we were having some challenges with *(fill in the blank)* that caused the company to *(fill in the blank with the actions taken by the company)* and institute new procedures to *(fill in the blank with new procedures)* which will actually cause *(fill in the blank with a benefit that the prospect will reap from these changes)*."

If you have heard an objection from many different prospects in the past, bring the issue up first and address it in your *Introductory Appointment-Setting Script*. When you bring up an objection first and address it, you not only eliminate the objection, you are able to position the objection the way that you want it to be perceived. This usually enables you to turn that objection from a negative into a positive.

Responding to Prospect Objections

No matter how articulate and persuasive you may be; no matter how carefully crafted your script; and even if you have tried to pre-empt every objection you can think of - you still more than likely will run into a few prospect objections.

These objections do not necessarily mean that your prospect does not want to meet with you. What they do mean is that the status quo is very powerful. In addition, people today are busier than they've ever been, and so an objection is frequently a 'knee jerk' way of saying they're busy. As you will discover later in this section, "I'm busy" is not a "no." It's a negotiation.

When you hear an objection your goal is to respond in such a way that you are able to keep your conversation on track and schedule the meeting. To begin, we have:

The Formula for Responding to Objections:

> **Agree with your prospect.**

Find a way to agree with your prospect, even if it's only to say, "I understand…" You will get nowhere arguing with your prospect. By agreeing, you put yourself on the prospect's side.

➤ **Reframe the objection.**

To "reframe" means to help redefine the way the prospect thinks about the objection. If you can get the prospect to look at their objections in a different way you have a much better chance of being able to schedule your appointment.

➤ **Ask for the meeting (*The Appointment-Setting Mantra*).**

After agreeing with your prospect and reframing the objection you must ask for the appointment again. Use *The Appointment-Setting Mantra.*

Sample Scripts for Responding to Prospect Objections

Here are sample scripts for dealing with some of the prospect objections that sales professionals hear most frequently:

We have a vendor/We're already working with someone.

You:

"I understand that you already have a vendor/are working with someone. You never know what may happen in the future, and right now I'd simply like to introduce myself and (*company name*). That way, if your situation changes you'll know me, you'll know (*company name*)…"

Then use *The Appointment-Setting Mantra* to ask for the

appointment again.

OR

"I understand that you already have a vendor/are working with someone. You never know what might happen in the future - it certainly never hurts to have another resource - and right now I'd simply like to introduce myself and (*company name*)."

Then use *The Appointment-Setting Mantra* to ask for the appointment again.

OR

"I understand that you already have a vendor/are working with someone. You never know what might happen in the future: perhaps you may need a resource to supplement what you are currently doing, and right now I'd simply like to introduce myself and (*company name*)."

Then use *The Appointment-Setting Mantra* to ask for the appointment again.

OR

Any combination of the above answers...

Then use *The Appointment-Setting Mantra* to ask for the appointment again.

We're not making any purchases/doing anything right now.

You:

"I understand that you aren't making any purchases/doing anything right now. That's great because right now I'd simply like to introduce myself and (*company name*). That way, in the future, when you're ready you'll know me and you'll know (*company name*)..."

Then use *The Appointment-Setting Mantra* to ask for the appointment again.

Send me information/Send me an e-mail.

This is an objection that prospects use when they mean something else. This objection hardly ever means that your prospect is going to sit down and read your materials when they arrive. Generally it means:

(a) You haven't convinced me,

or...

(b) I'm too busy.

Here, you want to get your prospect to reveal their true objection, which you can then address.

You:

"I have some information that I could put in the mail/e-mail to you. It's going to take you 10 minutes to read it and I only need 10 minutes whenever is good for you."

Then use *The Appointment-Setting Mantra* to ask for the appointment again.

OR

"I have some information that I could put in the mail/e-mail to you. However, I'm a walking, talking brochure/e-mail/web site and I only need 10 minutes whenever is good for you."

Then use *The Appointment-Setting Mantra* to ask for the appointment again.

Use a combination of the above two responses:

"I have some information that I could put in the mail/e-mail to you. However, it will take you 10 minutes to look through it and I only need 10 minutes whenever is good for you. I'm a walking, talking brochure/e-mail/web site."

Then use *The Appointment-Setting Mantra* to ask for the appointment again.

When you use one of these responses your prospect will usually reveal their true objection, which you can then address.

"Send information" most usually masks the next objection:

I'm too busy.

This is also an objection that means something else. "I'm too busy" is not a "no." Instead, think of this as a "yes"- you simply have to find the right time.

You:

"I understand that you're very busy. I only need 10 minutes of your time, whenever is good for you." *(Be sure to emphasize the word "whenever.")*

Then use *The Appointment-Setting Mantra* to ask for the appointment again. Make sure to offer different choices from the first time you asked for the meeting. Your prospect has already indicated that those times would not work.

OR

"I understand that you're very busy. When do you expect your time to free up - just a bit? *(Offer a couple of choices.)*

You tell me what looks good for you."

Then use *The Appointment-Setting Mantra* to ask for the appointment again. Make sure to offer different choices from the first time you asked for the meeting. Your prospect has already indicated that those times would not work.

OR

"I understand that you're very busy. Many of my prospects/ customers have said exactly the same thing and we were able to show them how they could save *(specify amount of time)* with *(fill in with your product/service)*. We only need 10-15 minutes of your time whenever is good for you and we could potentially save you *(specify amount of time)* so that you'd be able to focus on *(fill in with what else they could be doing)*.

Then use *The Appointment-Setting Mantra* to ask for the appointment again.

I'm too busy this week (or the next several weeks).

Your prospect has now given you an idea of when they might not be too busy. Use this information to schedule your appointment.

You:

"I understand that you're very busy. Let's pencil something in for *(the time frame mentioned by the prospect)*. It's not chiseled in stone. I'll call you to confirm and if it doesn't work out, we can always reschedule."

Then use *The Appointment-Setting Mantra* to ask for the appointment again. (And see *Chapter 6* for tips on *Following-up with Prospects*).

Call me back in two weeks (three weeks, four weeks, etc.).

You:

> "I'd be happy to - or you know what (*say this as if you just thought of it*), let's do this: let's pencil something in for (*time frame mentioned by prospect*) weeks from now. It's not chiseled in stone. I'll call you to confirm, and if it doesn't work out, we can always reschedule."

> Then use *The Appointment-Setting Mantra* to ask for the appointment again. (And see *Chapter 6* for tips on *Following-up with Prospects*.)

I'm not interested.

"I'm not interested" is not an objection. If you are repeatedly hearing "I'm not interested," the problem is either in your script or in your delivery, or both: prospects are telling you that you are not saying anything interesting.

The other possibility is that you are not speaking with a qualified prospect. If you are speaking with a qualified prospect, a good script with a stellar delivery will eliminate this issue.

If, however, every once in a while you hear this from a prospect, try these tactics:

You:

> "I understand that you're not interested. May I ask you why?"

> If you can get the prospect to talk with you they may give you valuable information that will help you engage their interest in you and your offer.

"Not interested? (*Said very softly and gently, and as if you are confused.*)

When you repeat a statement back to a prospect as a question it will frequently make the prospect explain their statement. That explanation may give you valuable information that will help you engage with the prospect.

Then, once you have engaged them, use *The Appointment-Setting Mantra* to ask for the appointment again.

So many sales people are calling.

Just like "I'm not interested," if you are hearing this, the problem is in your script or your delivery, or both: the prospect is telling you that you are not saying anything interesting.

The other possibility is that you are not speaking with a qualified prospect. If you are speaking with a qualified prospect, a good script with a stellar delivery will preempt this challenge.

If, however, every once in a while you hear this from a prospect, try this tactics:

You:

> I understand that you're very busy, and hear from a lot of companies. But it never hurts to have more choices - and right now I'd simply like to introduce myself and (*company name*). I only need 10 minutes of your time, whenever is good for you." *(Be sure to emphasize the word "whenever.")*

Then use *The Appointment-Setting Mantra* to ask for the appointment again.

I'll call you.

Sometimes a prospect will agree that a meeting is a good idea, but say that they are too busy to make an appointment now, and will call you (sometimes within a specified time frame). They will never call you - it is your job to call them.

You:

> "Great. And I know you're very busy, so I'll plan on touching base in (*the time frame the prospect has mentioned*) in case I haven't heard from you."

Chapter 5. Qualifying Your Prospect

You may be surprised to find the section on **Qualifying Your Prospect** at the end of the section on scripting. You may think you should put that in the first part of your script – but that would be a mistake that could cause your prospect to push back.

There are actually three steps to qualifying a prospect. Two of them take place before you ever speak with the prospect. Here is the formula for *Qualifying Your Prospect*:

> ➢ *Do your homework first.*
> ➢ *Identify the decision-maker.*
> ➢ *Ask for more information.*

First you must do your homework and make sure that your prospect meets the basic criteria that you have established for ideal prospects (see Part I on the importance of doing this). This is something that must happen before you get a prospect on the line. With so much information available online today, it's easier than ever to "prequalify" your prospects before you even pick up the telephone – and perhaps even more important is that your prospect will *expect* you to know these things about them.

Second, identify the highest-level person that you believe is the decision-maker. That person will either be the decision-maker or they will be able to point you in the right direction. You want to totally eliminate the need to ask the question, "Are you the person who makes the decision to purchase *(fill in product/ service)?*" If you are speaking with the head of a department or the owner of a company, you know you are speaking with someone who makes decisions.

The third step happens once you have your prospect on the phone: you may have some additional questions that you need to ask your prospect in order to determine that you are speaking with a qualified prospect.

Generally, a sales person's agenda on a prospecting call is to ask a lot of questions and then, given the correct answers, to schedule a meeting with the prospect.

The prospect, on the other hand, simply wants to know who you are and what you want.

These two desires clash – in fact, they are in total opposition to each other. In a conflict of interests like this, the prospect will always win by saying "I'm not interested" or by hanging up.

The answer to avoiding this clash

> **The prospect, on the other hand, simply wants to know who you are and what you want.**

of goals is to use the **Appointment-Setting Script Formula** to introduce yourself. Within that process, a conversation may develop that will allow you to ask questions and get some of the additional information that you need. Focus totally, however, **on scheduling the appointment**.

Once you actually have an appointment scheduled, the prospect is invested in the process, and is much more likely to answer your questions.

Once you have scheduled your appointment, continue *Qualifying Your Prospect* and ask your questions by using this simple script:

You:

> "So that I can prepare for our meeting, let me ask you a few questions."

Ask away – but be sure to only ask questions that you need answered in order to be certain you are speaking with a qualified prospect or that you really need to know to prepare for the meeting. Save everything else for your meeting (see *Part IV, Chapter 4* for the kinds of information-gathering questions you can use at a later stage in the sales process).

Chapter 6. Following-up with Prospects: The Instant Recap/Guilt Technique

Sometimes no matter how good your script is, how persuasive your delivery, or how well you are prepared to respond to objections, a prospect will insist that you call them back at a later date to schedule. This could be a couple of days to a couple of weeks to a couple of months – or beyond.

First make sure that you try "penciling in" a meeting for the future time mentioned by your prospect (see *Chapter 4* for this script.) About half of your prospects will agree to "pencil in" a meeting, eliminating the need for a call back.

If, however you are unable to convince your prospect to "pencil in" a meeting, it is important when calling your prospect back to be able to quickly and clearly remind them of your previous conversation and that they did indeed say they would meet you. If you are not able to accomplish that quickly, it is like completely starting over.

When you are able to quickly remind your prospect and re-establish your connection it is much easier to close on that appointment. That is why if your prospect asks you to call back another time to schedule the appointment, when you do call back you will want to use **The Instant Recap/Guilt Technique**:

You:

> "Hello, (*prospect's name*). This is (*your name*) with (*your company*). We spoke on (*date*) and you were (*repeat back the reason the prospect asked you to call back*) and you asked me to call you back and that you'd be able to carve out a few minutes for us to meet. So here I am. I'm calling you back. What does your calendar look like? Can we carve out a few minutes this week or is next week better?"

The "**Instant Recap**" part is:

> "We spoke on (*date*) and you were (*repeat back the reason the prospect asked you to call back*) and you asked me to call you back..."

By the way, if your prospect does not give you a reason they're asking you to call back later, such as "*I'm going on vacation,*" "*...in the middle of a project*" etc., you can simply say, "*...you were in the middle of a million things*" - which is sure to be true of anyone with whom you speak.

The "**Guilt Technique**" part is:

> "...you asked me to call you back and that you'd be able to carve out a few minutes for us to meet."

In combination, these tactics are very powerful. The *Instant Recap* brings the prospect back to the last conversation. Even if they don't remember your prior call, when you mention a date and the reason they asked you to call back, it is very clear that you have indeed, spoken with them before.

The *Guilt Technique* is the clincher. You are calling because they *asked you to* (and now they've put you to extra time and trouble).

Months can sometimes pass between the first contact with your prospect and the time they actually agree to meet with you. If this is your situation with a prospect (especially an important one) you might want to stay in touch with that prospect in between phone calls. See the *Sales Resource Guide* for recommendations on systems to automatically follow-up with prospects.

Chapter 7. Leveraging Appointments

There is a strategy that you can use to leverage the appointments you have already scheduled. The leverage can be within a particular prospect company; with competitor companies in an industry or in a region; or a combination of these.

Leveraging within a Prospect Company: If there is more than one prospect that you need to meet in a target company you can use the different prospects to leverage appointments.

Let's say for example that you want to meet with Jane Jones, Fred Smith and Rita White at XYZ Company. You start off by calling Rita:

You:

"I'm planning on meeting with Jane Jones and Fred Smith at your office and I would like to also stop by and introduce myself and (*company name/product/service*)."

Then go on with your script and use the *Appointment-Setting Mantra* to ask for the meeting.

You then call Jane and Fred, switch the names around, tell Jane that you're "planning on meeting with Fred and Rita" and tell Fred you're "planning on meeting with Jane and Rita."

Once you have an **anchor appointment**, that is, you successfully schedule a meeting with Fred, Rita or Jane, you will tweak your script slightly:

You:

"I will be meeting with Jane Jones at your office on (*date and time*) and I would like to also stop by and introduce myself and (*company name/product/service*)."

Then go on with your script and use the *Appointment-Setting*

Mantra to ask for the meeting.

Leveraging with competitor companies: This strategy also works within industries and in specific locations or regions. Let's say for example, you are going to be in Dallas and there are several restaurant chains that you would like to get into.

Call the first one and say:

You:

"I'm going to be in Dallas on *(date)* and I'm planning on meeting with Jane Jones of XYZ Restaurants. I would like to also stop by and introduce myself and *(company name/ product/service)* to you as well."

Then go on with your script and use the *Appointment-Setting Mantra* to ask for the meeting.

Once you have that first **anchor appointment** in Dallas with a prospect from a restaurant chain, you will tweak your script slightly:

You:

"I'm going to be in Dallas on *(date)* and I will be meeting with Jane Jones of XYZ Restaurants. I would like to also stop by and introduce myself and *(company name/product/service)* to you as well."

Then go on with your script and use the *Appointment-Setting Mantra* to ask for the meeting.

The idea that you are meeting with the competition or with others in their company gives you instant credibility, and creates those "I don't want to be left out" feelings within the prospect that will increase their desire to hear you out. You can use your appointments to help you get more appointments.

Part IV. When Your Entire Sale Takes Place Over the Telephone

In Part III, I emphasized that an *Appointment-Setting Script* is different from a script for when your entire sales process takes place over the phone. In this section, I will take you through scripts and tips for those who handle their entire sales process over the telephone.

Here is the sequence for that process:

➢ *Incoming Leads*
➢ *Gaining Agreement to Have a Selling Conversation*
➢ *Sample Scripts*
➢ *Questioning*
➢ *Answering Objections*
➢ *Answering Pricing Objections*
➢ *Multiple Decision-Makers and Influencers*
➢ *Following Up with Prospects*
➢ *Closing Scripts*

Chapter 1. Incoming Leads

Some sales professionals are in the lucky position of having leads come to them through the company web site, social media or other types of marketing activities. When these leads come in, however, it is just as important to be prepared as when you are making an initial prospecting call.

Too many sales professionals seem to think that if a lead is 'warm' they don't have to be as prepared or think in advance about what they are going to say. That is absolutely false. Although that lead may have contacted you, one misstep could mean losing the opportunity altogether. That is not a chance you want to take. It is imperative to be prepared with your script for when a prospect calls you.

The best way to proceed with incoming leads is to ask a lot of questions to gather information, qualify your prospect and move forward to the next step.

Script for Incoming Leads

You:

"Thank you so much for taking the time to contact us. What made you decide to pick up the phone and calls us?"

OR

"Thank you so much for taking the time to contact us. What was it about our website/webinar/teleconference/ promotion that made you decide to contact us?"

Additional Questions to Ask Incoming Leads

➤ **"What else/other solutions/programs/products/ services are you looking at?"**

You do not want to be blindsided. Just because a prospect called does not mean that they haven't also called your competitors.

➤ **"What have you seen so far that you like?"**

This is an important question. It will help you determine what the prospect needs and wants and where you are in relation to the competition.

➤ **"How long have you been considering this?"**

Another important question. If your prospect has been 'considering' for years they may not be a good prospect for you and/or you'll have to figure out how to get them to finally take action. That is why this next question is important, too:

➤ **"What has kept you from taking action so far?"**

This question will give you vital information to help you close. It will tell you why the prospect has not yet made a purchase. If you can eliminate the reason that they're not buying you should be able to get yourself a new customer.

> **"What is your timeline to decide?"**

   If your prospect's timeline is indefinite you'll have to give them a really good reason to make a decision to go with you now.

For more questions to add to your *Incoming Leads Script* see *Chapter 4.*

Chapter 2. Gaining Agreement to Have a Selling Conversation

When your entire sales process takes place over the telephone it follows a model that is very similar to beginning with a face-to-face appointment. When your goal is to set an appointment, you need agreement from your prospect to sit down together to have a conversation. When your entire sales process happens over the telephone, you still need agreement from your prospect to have that conversation.

In your face-to-face meeting you can ask your prospect all the questions you need to ask and give your prospect all of the information they need to make a buying decision. Likewise if your sale happens totally over the phone, once you have your prospect's agreement to have a selling conversation you are then in a position to ask your questions and give your prospect information.

The entire process hinges on getting the prospect's permission to proceed. The big difference is that when you are selling totally over the phone you can gain permission and then immediately have the selling conversation. *The Script Formula for Gaining Agreement to Have a Selling Conversation* is thus very similar to *The Script Formula for Appointment-Setting.*

The Script Formula for Gaining Agreement to Have a Selling Conversation

➢ **Introduce yourself.**

"Hello *(prospect name)*. My name is *(your name)*. I'm with *(company name)*."

➢ **One sentence sound bite that describes your company and the product/services you offer.**

"We are known for *(mention the outcome/benefit/results/ value that you/your company/product/service can bring to customers)*."

➢ **Position yourself as the expert/Mention Credentials.**

"We've been in business for/since *(number of years/date)* and work with *(name 2-3 customers)*."

➢ **Articulate benefits/Tell a Success Story.**

A Success Story *is a true story about a customer, their issue/ challenge and how you/your company/product/service were able to help. This should be 2-4 sentences maximum.*

➢ **Ask for what you want.**

"I'd like to speak with you for a few minutes about how we've been able to help our customers *(fill in the blank with the benefit or value.)* Do you have a few minutes right now?"

Then be quiet. Allow your prospect to respond. If the answer is "yes," go on with your questions and presentation. If the answer is 'no' use **The Appointment-Setting Mantra** *to schedule a phone date to continue the conversation:*

You:

"I understand that you don't have time right now. I need 10-15 minutes whenever is good for you. Can we carve out a few minutes later this morning or is this afternoon better?"

Offer a choice of times. Try to schedule this phone date as close to the time of the original phone call as possible. It is more difficult to get prospects to keep phone appointments then it is to get them to keep face-to-face appointments. Scheduling it soon after the original call increases the chances of actually connecting again with that decision-maker.

Chapter 3. Sample Scripts

Please note: These are samples – templates - only. You must use your own company credentials, statistics, customers and Success Stories.

Generic scripts do not work. The more specific that you are about your credentials, history and outcomes for customers, the more success you will have.

Script for Web Design Company

"Hello *(prospect name)*."

"My name is *(your name)* and I'm with *(company name)*. We're a web design and hosting company and we specialize in helping small business owners grow their business, make money and keep their customers happy."

"We've been in business for five years, we have more than 10,000 customers nationwide, and we work with small business owners all over the country."

"The bottom line is we make web technology accessible,

stress-free and revenue generating."

"For example: One of our customers, *(customer name)* wanted to increase revenue for his business. We developed a web site that gained him as many as 50 new customers a month and he's very happy."

"I'd like to speak with you for a few minutes about how we've been able to help our customers build additional revenue streams. Do you have a few minutes right now?"

Script for Printer/Graphic Arts Company

"Hello *(prospect's name)* my name is *(your name)* I'm with *(company name)*."

"We are a New York-based, full-service graphic arts company and our expertise is helping our customers save time and alleviate stress."

"We've been in business since *(year)* and we work with Company A, Company B and Company C..."

"The bottom line is: We deliver our work on time and on budget."

"We got a call a few weeks ago from a customer that needed a job done super fast. It was Thursday evening and he needed the job by Monday morning. So we stayed open on the weekend and got it to him by 8:00 a.m. that Monday. He was very relieved."

"I'd like to speak with you for a few minutes about your print needs and how we might be able to help. Do you have a few minutes right now?"

Once you have your prospect's agreement to have a conversation then you can proceed to ask relevant questions and offer relevant solutions.

Chapter 4. Questioning

Most sales people talk too much. The most important thing you can do is listen to your prospect. That's why I've included this chapter. Use the following questions to:

> ➢ qualify your prospect;
> ➢ gather important information;
> ➢ know how and when to follow up;
> ➢ differentiate yourself from the competition;
> ➢ help your prospect justify the purchase;
> ➢ gain agreement (especially on pricing in today's market), and…
> ➢ close the sale.

Qualifying Questions

The most important thing you can do is listen to your prospect.

It is crucially important to know how your prospect will make the decision. If you do not have this information, you may well miss a vital step that would make the difference between gaining a new account and losing it.

In addition, far too many sales professionals spend far too much time courting the wrong people. If you are not speaking with the Decision-Maker, you are not speaking with a qualified prospect. When you are not speaking with the Decision-Maker it lengthens your sales cycle and you risk losing the sale altogether. Too many sales professionals spend weeks, months, sometimes years chasing after prospects who finally come back to them and say, "My boss decided to go with someone else."

Don't let that happen to you. If you've started at the top as I previously recommended, the odds are excellent that you're speaking with a qualified prospect. Then ask the following questions to make sure that you are speaking with the decision-maker and you know how the decision will be made:

> "How will you be making this decision?"
> "What is your decision-making process?"
> "How have you made these decisions in the past?"
> "What are your criteria for evaluating this?"

In addition to *how*, it is crucially important to know *who* is going to be making the decision and to ensure that you know everyone who is involved in the decision.

> "Who other than yourself is involved in this decision?"
> "Who has the final say on this?"
> "Who is involved in this process?"
> "Who else is involved in this decision?"

It's always good to know how long the whole process will take and what the steps are in the process:

> "After we submit the proposal/the quote/the estimate/the information what happens next?"
> "What is your timeline for making this decision?"
> "How long is your decision-making process?"
> "When would you like to see a decision made on this?"
> "In the past, how long have these decisions taken?"

And of course, knowing what might stop the sale in its tracks:

> "What might stand in the way of that happening?"

Be sure to always ask these questions. Bottom line: If you are not speaking with the Decision-Maker you're not speaking with a qualified prospect. If you are not speaking with a qualified prospect the chances of closing your sale are slim to none.

Bottom line: If you are not speaking with the Decision-Maker you're not speaking with a qualified prospect.

Information-Gathering Questions

To close your sale you need to have a lot of information about your prospect, their challenges, their history, their expectations and desires. These questions are formulated to help you through the sales jungle:

> ### "What can you tell me about your organization... and yourself?"

This is an excellent place to start.

> ### "What can you tell me about the people involved in the process?"

Personalities can make a huge difference so the more you know about the people involved the stronger your position will be.

> ### "Who is your current/last vendor?"

It's important to know what's going on with your prospect. The past impacts the present.

> ### "Are you also asking them for pricing/a quote?"

Having this information will make sure there are no surprises.

> ### "Why are you considering using a different vendor/solution?"

This question will help you understand challenges and issues that affect your prospect. It's important information that will also help you understand their expectations and what is important to them.

> ### "What else/other companies/products/services are you considering?"

If you know your competition, you are better able to

position yourself to succeed.

> **"What are you looking to accomplish?"**

This question will help you understand your prospect's expectations. It will also help you know what will resonate with your prospect and whether or not you can help them.

> **"What is most important to you when making a decision to work with a vendor/company?"**

This is a key question. You need to know the criteria the prospect is using to make their decision. If you don't fit the criteria, you won't get the sale.

> **"What would the perfect solution/product/ service look like?"**

Another key question. You need to know the criteria the prospect is using to make their decision. If you don't fit the criteria, you won't get the sale.

> **"Why did you choose your current/last vendor/ product/service?"**

Knowing your prospect's decision-making process will help you understand where to go and what to do next.

> **"What has been your past experience?"**

If you can exploit a bad experience with a competitor, that's terrific. If the bad experience was with your company, you need to know about it and if possible, fix the problem.

> **"How do you know?"**

It's a good idea to know where your prospect is getting information and whether or not it's from a reliable source. (*Be very careful when you say this because you never want to make your prospect feel stupid.*)

> **"What else would you like to see?"**

This question can reveal other sales options for the prospect. This question could expand your sales.

> **"What do you like about what you're currently doing?"**

This question can be tricky. If you allow your prospect to linger here too long they may resell themselves on their current situation. You can, however, gather some important information to help you move your process forward.

> **"What don't you like about your current situation?"**

This question will give you vital information to help you assess your opportunity.

> **"What would you like to be enhanced or improved?"**

This is an important question to determine where opportunity exists.

> **"What can you tell me about your priorities?"**

This question will show you where your product or service fits in the queue of projects your prospecting currently focuses on.

> **"What prompted you to start this project now?"**

Timing is everything. Understand your prospect's situation and you'll learn what you need to help them and close the sale.

> **"What would need to happen for you to choose us as your vendor/provider/solution?"**

This question will help you know realistically if this sale is something that you can accomplish.

Differentiating Questions

It is always bad form to bad mouth the competition. There is nothing the matter, however, with pointing out the competition's weaknesses. If you know of certain weaknesses of the prospect's current vendor you can ask:

> ➤ **"When (*fill in the blank*) happens, how do you handle it?"**

> Fill in the blank with the situation/problem that the current vendor is either unable to handle or handles poorly. This will get the prospect talking about their current situation and the problems they are having, and give you a chance to talk about how you/your company/ product/service do things differently and potentially how you can help them.

> ➤ **"What are you doing about (*fill in the blank*)?"**

> Again, fill in the blank with the situation/problem that the current vendor is either unable to handle or handles poorly. This will get the prospect talking about their current situation and the problems they are having, and give you a chance to talk about how you/your company/ product/service do things differently and potentially how you can help them.

In a similar way, if you know that your prospect is considering the competition, ask:

> ➤ **"What will you do when (*fill in the blank*) happens?"**

> You fill in the blank, of course, with a situation/ problem that your competitor is either unable to handle

or handles poorly. This will get the prospect talking about their current situation and the problems they are having, and give you a chance to talk about how you/ your company/product/service do things differently and potentially how you can help them.

Clarifying The Next Steps

It is imperative to understand your prospect's process. When having a conversation with a prospect, whether on the telephone or face-to-face, always conclude your conversation by asking a *Next Step* question:

> ➤ **"After our conversation (*discussion/you see our presentation...*) if you see that our product/service is a perfect fit for you, what would happen next?"**
>
> Any answer other than the prospect would be ready to move forward means that you have more work to do to close the sale.

> ➤ **"What happens next?"**
>
> To be ahead of the game, you always need to know the next step in your prospect's buying process.

> ➤ **"What is the next step?"**
>
> To be ahead of the game, you always need to know the next step for your prospect's buying process.

> ➤ **"How should we proceed?"**
> A variation of the question above.

Justifying The Purchase

Prospects need a reason to buy. You want to help them find that reason and justify the decision by asking key questions, many of which create increasing motivation and justification for the decision to change their current situation.

Here are some questions to accomplish that:

> **"How often does that happen?"**

This question helps prospect see the larger picture. It helps create justification for change.

> **"Then what do you have to do?"**

Ask this after getting the answer to the question above. This creates more motivation and justification for change. Then ask the following questions, which reinforce that motivation and justification:

> **"How long has it been going on?"**

> **"How much does it cost you?"**

> **"How much time does it take now?"**

> **"How is it being handled now?"**

> **"How will you handle it?"**

The idea here is to get the prospect talking about how difficult the whole situation is. This creates more motivation and justification for change.

> **"What other problems does that cause?"**

Ask these questions after the ones above, to continue the sequence for motivation and justification for change.

> **"What else happens?"**

> **"How did you/your employees/your customers react?"** *OR...*

> **"How does that make them feel?"**

> **"How does that make you feel?"**

> **"How will you prevent it from happening again?"**

Now continue with the following sequence for motivation and justification for the purchase.

➤ **"How do you feel you would use this product/service?"**

➤ **"What do you feel that would do for you?"**

➤ **"Would you see this as something that would help you avoid those problems in the future?"**

If your prospect answers "yes" to this, it will help them justify the purchase even more. Not only will the product/service help now, it will help in the future.

➤ **"How much do you think this would help you make?"**

This question justifies expense. Use this question, or depending on the circumstances, the following question:

➤ **"How much do you think this would help you save?"**

This question also helps justify expense.

➤ **"What would motivate you to change?"**

This question creates the rationale a prospect will use to justify their purchase.

Finally, always ask the following two questions so that you'll have the full range of the prospect's budget and motivation. (See *Gathering Budget Information* in this chapter, for more on this critical subject.)

Some people are motivated by a positive outcome while others are motivated by avoiding a negative consequence. These two questions together cover both:

➤ **"How much would it be worth to you to solve this problem?"**

This question reveals a prospect's motivation. If it's not worth much to them to solve the problem, you probably won't get the sale.

> **"What would it cost, ultimately, if things remained the same?"**

This question helps the prospect justify the purchase. The two questions together will help you determine a prospect's budget.

Gaining Agreement

When speaking with a prospect it is always important to 'take their pulse' to find out what they are thinking and feeling. As with the preceding steps in the sales process, the best way to do this is to ask questions.

These are different questions, however, from the information-gathering ones. Most of these questions are 'yes' or 'no' questions. If your presentation is going well you'll be getting a 'yes' each time, and that will move your prospect toward their final agreement to buy. If you get a 'no,' ask more questions. You're going in the wrong direction!

> **"Are you with me on this?"**

> **"Does that make sense?"**

> **"Is this what you're looking for?"**

> **"Can you see the benefit of this?"**

> **"Will this fit your situation?"**

> **"What do you think so far?"**

> **"How does that sound?"**

These are 'check-in' questions: they let you know where you are with your prospect. Check in periodically, because if you're off track you want to know so you can make adjustments.

One more important 'check-in' question:

> **"Do you have a preference?"**

   If your prospect has a preference, you need to know what it is and how they arrived at that preference. Having a preference also moves the prospect one step closer to saying "yes."

Gathering Budget Information

Of course, it's especially important for you to determine whether a prospect has the budget to make the purchase. A prospect without a budget is probably not a great prospect - at least at that moment in time. The simplest approach is to ask:

> **"What is your budget for this?"**

   This is a totally reasonable question that many sales professionals neglect to ask either because they forget or because they are uncomfortable asking.

Sometimes prospects will balk if you ask, "What is your budget for this?" – so an alternative is to ask:

> **"Ballpark, what is your budget for this?"**

   This phrasing is important. By adding the word, 'ballpark," you can help the prospect feel they are not giving you highly specific information and that they won't be held to a number. This phrasing makes it easier for your prospect to answer the question.

> **What does that include?**
   This is an important question because you need to be able to understand the budget figure that your prospect

provides. If it's a budget, but not for the type of thing you're selling, you'll have a problem. Clarify this early on.

> **"What was your budget last time?"**

If your prospect does not have a budget, but has had one for such purposes in the past, this can give you an idea of how important they feel this type of purchase is. It can also act as a guideline to help them set their new budget. In fact, if you get into the prospect's process early enough you might be in a position to help them set their budget. That's a great place to be!

The next stage is to move from the potential budget to the actual price points that will make this sale possible.

> **"How do you handle budget considerations?"**

This is a variation of the questions above. You must ask enough of these questions until you have a handle on your prospect's budget.

> **"How will the funding for the project be justified?"**

Sometimes straightforward is the best approach. If you need more information, ask more questions.

> **"How much support does this have at the executive level?"**

This is a very important question if you are dealing with someone who is farther down the chain of command. You do not want to invest time and resources only to hear, "My boss said 'no.'"

Gaining Agreement on Pricing

➤ **"Does this work for your budget?"**

An important checking-in question. If the answer is 'no' you'll have to do more digging and/or more selling on value.

➤ **"Is this what you're looking to spend?"**

Another checking-in variation. Again, if the answer is 'no' you'll have to do more digging and/or more selling on value.

➤ **"If you were comfortable that this solution/ product/service is the answer, would (*price*) work for you?"**

This is a fabulous question: you're getting agreement on pricing, a frequent sticking point, before you get agreement on the actual solution/product/service. In other words, you're getting the hard part out of the way first.

➤ **"Which of these price points would work for you?"**

Multiple choices. Let the prospect choose. Start with the highest price, then the middle price, than the lowest. Bear in mind that most of the time your prospect will pick the one in the middle. Price accordingly.

Pre-Closing Questions

I call these 'pre-closing' questions because while the answer to any one of these questions is not the final close, when you get the right answers to these questions you're pretty darn close:

➤ **"How can we make this work?"**

➤ **"How can we make this happen?"**

- ➤ "How can we get approval?"

- ➤ "How would you like to proceed?"

- ➤ "How do you see us proceeding?"

- ➤ "How can we be the ones that you'll choose?"

- ➤ "How can we be part of the bidding process?"

Closing Questions

Finally, there are many ways in which to clinch the deal. Ask any of these Closing Questions, and if you get a 'yes,' you have closed. Stop selling!

- ➤ "Are you ready to get started?"

- ➤ "Shall I draw up a contract?"

- ➤ "Shall we finalize the details?"

- ➤ "When would you like to get started?"

- ➤ "Should we go ahead and finalize the details?"

- ➤ "Which plan do you want to go with?"

- ➤ "Do you want plan A or plan B?"

- ➤ "How about starting out with a trial order?"

- ➤ "How soon can we get started?"

- ➤ "How about starting now?"

- ➤ "How many do you want to start with?"

- ➤ "How fast will you need this?"

➤ **"How much will you need to start off with?"**

➤ **"How do you want to pay for this?"**

➤ **"How do you want this delivered?"**

Chapter 5. Answering Objections

Of course, before that glorious moment of closing the sale, it's possible that your prospect will voice objections.

As I said in Part III, the very best way to deal with prospect objections is to pre-empt them: to address them before the prospect ever brings them up. If there are common objections that you frequently hear, you are much better off addressing those up front in your script. This is an incredibly powerful way to minimize the number of objections your prospect might raise.

By now, of course, I hope you've learned those *(appointment-setting) Scripts for Responding to Prospect Objections* by heart, but when your entire sale takes place over the telephone, it's especially important to be well-prepared to answer any objections that you might hear later in the sales process, too.

Be prepared, and follow these **Four Steps for Handling Objections:**

1. **Be sure that you understand what your prospect's objection really means.**

   For example: Objection: "It's too expensive."

   > Could mean:
   > ➤ "I'm not the decision-maker."
   > ➤ "I do not have the budget right now."
   > ➤ "I do not see the value."

   In order to ensure that you understand the objection, ask:

   You:
   > "Could you clarify that please?"

   OR

   > "Can you help me understand what *(prospect's objection)* means?"

   You can also repeat back the prospect's objection **gently, and sounding a little confused**. This will generally make your prospect explain what they mean. Be careful with this. You do not want to sound angry or defensive, or as though you are criticizing your prospect.

2. **Isolate the objection.**

   You:
   > "Aside from *(prospect's objection)*, what else might keep you from saying yes?"

3. **Make sure it is the only objection – or that you know them all.**

You:

"Aside from (*prospect's first objection and prospect's second objection*) what else might keep you from saying 'yes' today?"

Keep asking:

You:

"Anything else?"

Keep asking until you are sure that you have heard all of your prospect's objections, and then:

4. Eliminate the objection(s).

Once you are sure of the objection(s), and that you know all the barriers to agreement, then, and only then, address them.

Common Objections

I don't have the money.

You:

"I understand that you do not have the money right now. Leaving money aside for a moment, if you had the money, would you want to move forward?"

OR

"I understand that you do not have the money right now. Aside from this issue, what else might stand in the way of you moving forward?"

If the responses you are getting are that the prospect would buy if money was not the issue, you now have options - and they are options other than lowering your price. You could work out a payment plan; help the prospect obtain financing; or help the prospect figure out where they could find the money.

I have to speak with my husband/wife/ significant other/business partner.

You:

> "I understand that you have to speak with your husband/ wife/significant other/business partner. If this was up to you alone, would you want to move forward?"

> **OR**

> "I understand that you have to speak with your husband/ wife/significant other/business partner. Let's go ahead and fill out the paperwork and when your husband/wife/ significant other/business partner says 'ok,' we'll be ready to go. If not, I'll tear it up."

I'm not interested.

As I said in Part III, "I'm not interested" is not an objection. If you are repeatedly hearing "I'm not interested," the problem is either in your script or in your delivery, or both: prospects are telling you that you are not saying anything interesting.

The other possibility is that you are not speaking with a qualified prospect. If you are speaking with a qualified prospect, a good script with a stellar delivery will eliminate this issue.

If, however, you are hearing this only occasionally, try the following:

You:

> "I understand that you're not interested in *(name of product/service)*. I wouldn't expect you to be as you are just hearing of it. I do know that you are interested in (fill in the benefit)." *(Continue with your script.)*

OR

"I understand. Many of my customers have said the same thing and then once they found out about how *(name of product/service)* is able to help *(fill in the benefit)* they were glad they took time." *(Continue with your script.)*

OR

"Not interested?" *(Be sure to sound gently confused and make sure that your tone is not at all threatening or disbelieving. You instead want to sound as though you are confused but very, very interested.)*

Frequently when you repeat a prospect's words back to them in this manner they will start explaining what they mean. You may get some vital information that will enable you to continue the conversation and help you make a sale.

Send Me Information/An Email.

You:

"I'd be happy to, and first let's make sure that you are ready to act when you receive the information." *(Ask your qualifying questions.)*

OR

"I'd be happy to. What do you need to see in order to be able to make a decision?"

OR

"I'd be happy to. Once you receive the information/email and assuming that you like what you see/read, when will you make the decision?"

OR

"I'd be happy to. By the way, what other solutions/ companies/products/information are you looking at?"

"What do you like so far?"

"What has stopped you from taking action on that?"

THEN

"I'll get this out to you today. Let's set up a time to speak further about this. Do you have time on *(fill in the date)* or is *(fill in the date)* better?"

Always try to schedule a time to continue the conversation. Use the *Appointment-Setting Mantra.* If, however, you are not able to schedule a phone date:

You:

"When should I check back with you?" *(Offer choices of times.)*

THEN

When you call back, if your prospect says:

I looked at it and I'm not interested.

You:

"I understand. Many of our customers don't get the full picture from the brochure/the web site/email. Let's do this, I'll take a few minutes to explain how we're helping our customers and how it might help you and after our conversation if you still think it's not a fit then I'll understand."

I want to think about it.

You:

"I understand that you need to think about this. From what we've already discussed, you do understand how this product/service works, right?"

"And this does fit within your budget, correct?"

"And you do understand the value of getting/achieving *(a benefit that you know the prospect wants)* today/soon, right?"

"OK, great. So I'm not clear, what have I missed? What do you need to think about?"

OR

"(Prospect's name), when I tell someone 'I want to think about it,' for me that usually means either 'I don't understand' or 'I'm not sold yet.' Which is it for you?"

OR

"Certainly, I understand that you need to think about this. To clarify my thinking, are you concerned about the quality? Are you concerned that it's not the right fit? Are you concerned…" *(Keep asking questions until you are able to figure out the exact area of concern and can respond to that. Then ask for the sale again.)*

I'm already working a vendor/supplier.

You:

"I understand that you're already working with someone and we'd like to start out as a backup. In order for you to feel perfectly comfortable that we can handle your needs I'm going to suggest that you give us a small order in order for us to prove our worth to you. I'm not asking you to switch to us, simply give us a chance to show you what we can do with a small order and this will give you a chance to do the comparison. After a few months, you'll be the judge. I can get this out to you right away: you'll have it by the beginning of the week or is midweek better?"

Chapter 6. Answering Pricing Objections

Most sales professionals treat pricing objections as something that happens at the end of the sales process. They look for responses that will take the pricing objection away.

Eliminating pricing objections, however, is a process that starts from the very beginning of your first conversation with a prospect. If you wait till the end of the process, more than likely you will lose the sale.

From the very beginning of your sales process, in every interaction that you have with a prospect you want to ensure that:

1. You are speaking with a qualified prospect.
2. Your prospect understands the value that your product/service represents.
3. Your prospect is in agreement with your assessment of that value.

If you are not speaking with a qualified prospect, that prospect will not buy from you. If your prospect does not have the budget (and will never have the budget), that prospect will not buy from you. That is why it is so imperative to ask the right questions. Study *Part IV, Chapter 4* and use all of the qualifying and information-gathering questions you find there.

Don't be afraid to ask the tough questions.

Don't be afraid to ask the tough questions. Many sales people fear rejection, and that is why they put off asking the bottom-line questions that can cross a prospect off their list. You are in a much better position, however, if you find out early on that a given prospect is not a good one for you. Spending weeks or months (or years) chasing someone who is not a viable prospect will simply make you frustrated and angry – and waste time and effort that could be invested in cultivating real prospects.

Make sure that your prospect understands the value that your product/service represents. You will do this best if you deeply understand your prospect's issues and concerns, and that means listening carefully, asking information-gathering questions, and then finding ways to tie your offering to solving their challenges.

In *Part III, The Introductory Appointment-Setting Script,* I talked about pre-empting objections. You must set the stage early, so that the prospect sees your offering more clearly.

If, for example, your product/service is more expensive than some others, you want them to know why that is. Perhaps your company uses superior quality products in manufacturing, or offers a special level of service above and beyond what the competition offers. You will want to bring that up yourself, as an added value:

> "Our product/service is certainly not the cheapest. That's because we use superior quality materials and offer 24/7 service. None of our competitors can say that."

By addressing the objection before it is even voiced, you turn a negative into a positive.

Another example: Let's say that your company has been having service issues and that these problems are widely known. You're certain that your prospect knows about the issues and will see them as a significant negative. If the issues have been corrected or are in the process of being corrected you should bring those issues up early in your script:

> "While we were having some challenges with *(fill in the blank),* that caused the company to *(fill in the blank with the actions taken by the company)* and institute new procedures to *(fill in the blank with new procedures)* which will actually cause *(fill in the blank with a benefit that the prospect will reap from these changes)."*

As in the previous example, here you can turn a negative into a positive.

When you bring up an objection first and address it this way, you are in a far more powerful position. You not only eliminate the objection, you are able to frame the way that you want it to be perceived. Pre-empting objections will enable you to turn the prospect's view of these issues from a negative into a positive one.

Make sure that your prospect agrees that your offering will help and/or solve their challenges. Check in frequently with your prospect and get that prospect 'on board' with what you are discussing. Use the questions in *Part IV, Chapter 4*, for gaining agreement. Don't mistake a prospect's silence for agreement. You must ask.

In addition, prospects need a reason to buy. You want to help them find that reason and justify the decision by asking questions that create the increasing motivation to change their current situation, and justification for the decision to buy.

In *Part IV,* I have given you a long, long list of these types of questions. Here are a few examples: for a complete list, with explanations of their use, see *Part IV, Chapter 4:*

> **"How often does that happen?"**

> **"Then what do you have to do?"**

> **"How long has it been going on?"**

> **"How much does it cost you?"**

> **"How much time does it take now?"**

> **"What other problems does that cause?"**

> **"Would you see this as something that would help you avoid those problems in the future?"**

➤ **"How much do you think this would help you make?"**

➤ **"How much do you think this would help you save?"**

Always ask the following two questions to define the full range of the prospect's budget and motivation.

➤ **"How much would it be worth to you to solve this problem?"**

This question reveals a prospect's motivation. If it's not worth much to them to solve the problem, you probably won't get the sale.

➤ **"What would it cost, ultimately, if things remained the same?"**

This question helps the prospect justify the purchase. The two questions together will help you determine a prospect's budget.

Bottom line: If your prospect does not see the value, and/or it's not that much of an issue, you will not get the sale.

Bottom line: If your prospect does not see the value, and/or it's not that much of an issue, you will not get the sale.

Once you have helped your prospect justify the purchase, you want to help that prospect agree on the pricing of your offer. Use these questions:

Gaining Agreement on Pricing

➤ **"Does this work for your budget?"**

An important checking-in question. If the answer is 'no'

you'll have to do more digging and/or more selling on value.

> **"Is this what you're looking to spend?"**

Another checking-in variation. Again, if the answer is 'no' you'll have to do more digging and/or more selling on value.

> **"If you were comfortable that this solution/ product/service is the answer, would (*price*) work for you?"**

This is a fabulous question: You're getting agreement on pricing, a frequent sticking point, before you get agreement on the actual solution/product/service. In other words, you're getting the hard part out of the way first.

> **"Which of these price points would work for you?"**

Multiple choices. Let the prospect choose. Start with the highest price, then the middle price, than the lowest. Bear in mind that most of the time your prospect will pick the one in the middle. Price accordingly.

Sometimes in spite of your best efforts, you will encounter a pricing objection, such as "It's too expensive" or "I don't have the budget" or "We're not making any purchases/doing anything right now."

If that does happen, remember to first make sure that you understand what the prospect means by that objection. Ask:

"Would you clarify that for me, please?"

Once you are sure that you understand your prospect, then you must *Isolate the Objection,* as discussed in *Part IV, Chapter 5, Answering Objections.*

I don't have the budget.

You:

> "I understand that you don't have the budget right now. Leaving that aside for a moment, if you had the budget, would you want to move forward?"

OR

> "I understand that you do not have the budget right now. Aside from this issue, what else might stand in the way of you moving forward?"

If the responses you are getting are that the prospect would buy if budget was not the issue, you now have options - and they are options other than lowering your price. You could work out a payment plan; help the prospect obtain financing; or help the prospect figure out where they could find the budget.

We're not making any purchases/doing anything right now.

You:

> "I understand that you're not making any purchases/doing anything right now. If the timing/your situation were different would you see this product/service as the solution?"

You want to be sure that nothing else stands in the way, that if the timing or situation were different, your product/service would be what your prospect wants. Once you have isolated the objection and are sure there are no other objections, then ask some questions:

> ➤ **"What other budget line could cover this?"**

> ➤ **"What happens when you have to make**

emergency purchases?"

> **"Who else might be interested in this that also has a budget?"**

> **"Who else has the authority to purchase this?"**

Help your prospect strategize a way to make the purchase.

The Dollars and Sense

Another way to overcome pricing objections is to help your prospect calculate the value and/or the savings. As I mentioned earlier in this chapter, asking questions is the key. If your product or service helps a prospect ultimately save money, help them calculate the exact amount of money they would save and how long it might take them to save it. Be specific.

A good basic example of this might be a 'pay as you go' phone. Someone might have a phone like this because they do not want to pay the monthly charges associated with a cell phone. Making calls, however, might cost them between $.25-$.50/minute. If they make enough calls, they may actually be spending more than the monthly cell phone fee. Do these calculations with your prospect.

Ask:

> **"How much are you currently spending on** (fill in product/service)**?"**

> **"How often do you use** (fill in product/service)**?"**

Then say,

You:

"Let's figure this out together. Do you have a pen and paper?"

OR

"Do you have a calculator?"

Then walk your prospect through the math.

Make sure to include the prospect's (or their team's) time in your calculations. Many prospects will not take this into consideration - so it's your job to ensure that they do.

Ask your prospect:

You:

"You're probably making (*dollar amount*)/hour (*make sure to overestimate what you think the person might be making*), what does that come out to monthly?"

"How much time are you spending on (*fill in with the activity*)?"

Then do the math with your prospect: *(dollar amount)*/hour X time spent = Value of Prospect's Time.

Doing these types of calculations with your prospects will go a long way toward overcoming pricing objections.

Lowering the Price (a last resort).

The problem with this script is that far too many sales professionals are too willing to drop the price too quickly. Only do this if there is no other option - and never, ever give the full amount of the product/service for a lower price. You always need to eliminate something if you are going to drop the price.

You:

"I understand that you don't have it in your budget right now. You've said that if you had the budget you would want to move on this, correct?" *(Wait for the answer. The prospect must say 'yes' before you proceed.)*

THEN

"We might be able to do it without *(name two or three features that you can take out)*..."

OR

"We might be able to start with a smaller order of *(smaller order than previously discussed)*..."

THEN

"I'll have to check it with my manager. If I can get the ok on this are you ready to proceed?" *(Again, wait for the answer. The prospect must say 'yes' before you proceed.)*

"That's great. Let me put you on hold for a moment while I go ask my manager." *(Put the prospect on hold for 30 seconds or so then come back on the line and close your sale.)*

Adding Value (one more last resort).

Use this only as a last resort when other attempts have failed:

You:
"You really know how to drive a hard bargain - so we can give you *(fill in an extra)* if you give me the go ahead right now. How is that?"

OR

"You really know how to drive a hard bargain - I like that. Just to show you how much I'm willing to give and how much I want your business, I'm going to give you my personal, direct line so that you don't ever have to worry about dealing with a switchboard or secretary or not getting through. Only my best clients have my direct dial. How do you want to pay for this? Credit card or company check?"

Chapter 7. Multiple Decision-Makers and Influencers

I want to repeat my earlier statement: "if you're not speaking with the decision-maker, you're not speaking with a qualified prospect." Sometimes, however, you reach the decision-maker only to be told to speak with someone else first, or you learn that there are many people involved in the decision.

If you have a good script that is written specifically for the level of the decision-maker and that focuses on appropriate issues for that level, you will almost never be pushed down the chain of command. If this does happen, however, before you call that second in command be sure to ask:

> "If I can show *(name of second in command)* the value of our program/product/ solution and she is convinced of that value and wants to move forward with us - will you sign off on that decision?"

By asking this question you are getting the decision-maker's agreement before you speak with the second in command, putting you in a much more favorable and much stronger position.

Sometimes, there are multiple decision-makers, people who might make the decision on their piece of the puzzle but who do not ultimately sign off on the entirety of the project. These people are called *"Influencers."*

Sometimes a prospect will tell you they are the decision-maker, yet they also need to have 'buy-in' from other executives. Even a CEO may need buy-in from top executives who will be implementing a particular program, so it is imperative to know early on everyone who will be involved.

The way to ensure you have all the information about this that you need at the start of your sales process is to ask questions. As in Chapter 4 ask:

> **"Who other than yourself is involved in this decision?"**

> **"Who has the final say on this?"**

> **"Who is involved in this process?"**

> **"Who else is involved in this decision?"**

> **"How have you made these decisions in the past?"**

> **"How are these decisions usually made?"**

Once you know all the people involved in the process and their part in the process, the next step is to try to schedule a conference call with all of them. Say to your main contact:

> "Let's put together a brief conference call with you and *(names of the other people involved)* so that they can get an overview of what's happening and we can decide next steps."

If your main contact is unwilling to do this, it could be a sign that he/she is simply not that interested.

When your main contact agrees to the conference call, ask that contact to set it up.

> "Since they already know you, would you be good enough to coordinate a time for all of us to connect on a teleconference?"

Then spend time with your contact to shape the agenda. After your conference call you may have the opportunity to speak with the other decision-makers/influencers individually. If you do, make sure to ask each and every one:

> "If it were up to you alone, would you move forward on this?"

If the answer from that prospect is, "no," you have more work to do with that prospect. When there are multiple people involved in a decision, sometimes one negative can tank the entire deal, so watch out for this.

If you are not able to have the conversation with each of the decision-makers/influencers, set up a time to speak again with your main contact and ask:

> "How are the others feeling about *(your offering)*? What do you see as our next steps?"

This will tell you how things stand and how to proceed.

Sometimes, no matter how hard you have tried, you are unable to reach the decision-maker directly. There are some selling situations where for whatever reason you are speaking with someone lower down the chain of command, someone who cannot make a decision, but who has access to the decision-maker and influence on their decision.

In this situation, you will want to coach the *Influencer* to help them sell you/your product/service. Ideally what you want is for that person to facilitate your conversation with the decision-maker.

When dealing with an *Influencer*, as I've emphasized throughout this handbook, asking questions is vital. Here are some important ones to start out:

> ➢ **"How much support does this have at the executive level?"**

> ➢ **"What issues/challenges are facing your boss *(Manager/Vice President, etc.)*?"**

> ➢ **"How do you think your boss *(Manager/Vice President, etc.)* will respond to this product/service/program?"**

> **"What do you think your boss (*Manager/Vice President, etc.*) will like about this product/ service/program?"**

> **"What do you think your boss (*Manager/Vice President, etc.*) will dislike about this product/ service/program?"**

Gather as much information as you can about the decision-maker, the process and anything else that you can find out. Ask that *Influencer* to help you:

> "I'm wondering if you can help me. Would you be good enough to facilitate a brief conversation with your boss (Manager/Vice President, etc.) to discuss how we might help *(fill in with the benefit)*?"

Depending on the situation at your prospect company, your *Influencer* may be more or less willing to help you. This is also the problem with starting too low in the chain of command: it can be difficult to move up to having the conversation with the person who will actually sign off on the deal. That is why you always want to start with the highest-level person who you believe is the decision-maker.

That is why you always want to start with the highest-level person who you believe is the decision-maker.

That said, if you are not able to convince your *Influencer* to move you further up the chain of command, try this last resort: tell your contact that your boss is giving you a hard time. Tell the *Influencer* that although you value your relationship with him/her and do understand that he/she is the best person to talk to, your boss is demanding that you speak with their boss.

You:

> "*(Influencer's name)*, I'm hoping that you can help me. I'm in a really tough spot - I just had a conversation with my manager. She/He found out that I'd never had a conversation with *(real decision-maker's name)* and he/she's insisting that I call *(real decision-maker's name)* immediately. I tried to explain that you really are the person we need to be speaking with, but my boss was just so angry with me that she/he wouldn't let me explain.
>
> "I really value our relationship and don't want to do anything to jeopardize it... that's why I've come to you first, before doing anything. I'm hoping that you can help facilitate a brief conversation with your boss (*Manager/Vice President, etc.*) Can you help me?"

Sometimes this will work to move you up the chain. If it does not - if your *Influencer* will not help - then say:

You:

> "Well, ok. I'll hold off as long as I can. I'm in a really tough spot – I really do not want to jeopardize our relationship in any way, but if my manager keeps insisting that I contact *(real decision-maker's name)* I'm going to have to do it. I won't have any choice, but I wanted to let you know what's going on first."

At that point you can make the decision whether or not to call the real decision-maker directly. And, unfortunately, this approach will not work if you do not have a boss on whom to lay the blame.

Chapter 8. Following-up with Prospects

If your sale has not yet closed and you need to have another conversation with your prospect, be sure that you have both agreed on next steps and then be sure to say:

You:
> "Let's set up a time to continue our conversation. *(Pick a date based on the conversation you've had and the time line discussed.)* Would *(date)* work for you or would *(date)* be better?"

You are always better off scheduling a date and time for your next conversation. If your prospect is unable or unwilling to schedule a phone date, then ask:

You:
> "When should I check back with you?"

Your prospect will give you some time frame (say, "two weeks"), and you should be sure to do exactly what your prospect requests - simply doing it a little earlier. That is, if your prospect asks you to call back in two weeks, call in a week and a half. If your prospect asks you to call back in two months, call back in a month and a half. It is always better to be too early for an opportunity than to be too late.

When you call back, once you get the prospect on the line use *The Instant Recap/Guilt Technique*, as outlined in *Part III, Chapter 6* under *Following-up with Prospects:*

You:
> "Hello *(prospect name)*. This is *(your name)* with *(your company)*. We spoke on *(date)* and discussed *(fill in what you discussed)*. Our next step was to *(fill in the next step)* and you asked me to call you back to *(fill in the reason for the phone call)*."

It is important when calling your prospect back to be able to quickly and clearly remind them of your previous conversation and that they did indeed ask you to call again. When you are able to quickly re-establish your connection it is much easier to close.

As I said before, the *Guilt Technique* is the clincher. You are calling because they *asked you to* (and now they've put you to extra time and trouble). And by reminding them of that you were on the verge of the *next step*, you may get them to move forward.

Following up on information/email sent

During the course of your conversation with a prospect, that prospect might have asked you to forward information either via email or through the postal service before they will actually order. Here is a script that you can use to follow-up with prospects after you have sent them information:

You:
> "I'm sure you've reviewed the information/email/web site/brochure and liked what you saw - as most people do. Did you want to start with *(size of order)* or *(bigger order)?*"

Provide value when you call

Far too many sales professionals follow-up with prospects with lame phrases like these: "I'm just calling to touch base," or "I'm just calling to check in," or, "I'm just calling to stay in touch to see if you need anything."

Customers will frequently view these no-substance calls as annoying or a nuisance. Make it your policy that every time you call you have a value-related reason for doing so. Industry or product-related news, upcoming promotions or ideas that you believe they could use – all these are good reasons to call your prospects and/or customers.

Make it your policy that every time you call you have a value-related reason for doing so.

Ask yourself the question: "What information could I give my prospect or customer that would make them glad that I called?" Proceed accordingly.

A big part of being effective in sales is being sure you always know what's going on with your top prospects and customers. When you know about the significant events that are affecting them and their businesses, you will have excellent reasons to stay in touch.

There is now a very handy tool that you can use to know what is going on with your top customers and prospects. It will give you the inside scoop and notify you of the right times to get in contact. It will give you ideas of topics you should mention. This nifty tool is Google Alerts.

Google Alerts allows you to enter the names of your prospects or customers as search terms. Google will then search for those prospect and customer names and send you emails whenever one is mentioned anywhere on the Web. Anytime there is news about your top customers or prospects, you will know.

You can choose how often you would like to receive the alerts: as they happen, once a day, once a week. The Google emails will contain links to the actual articles so that you can read what is said about your customers and prospects. This will give you ample clues as to what to say when you contact them.

To set up Google Alerts, go to:
http://www.google.com/alerts?hl=en&gl=us.

To manage your alerts, you will need to set up an account with Google. There is no charge for this service and you can use your existing e-mail address.

Ask your customers why they buy

This is a really simple idea but it's something that most sales professionals never do. Knowing the reason that your customers buy from you is very powerful. This knowledge will help in two ways:

- you will be able to continue providing appropriate value to that customer.

- this information will help you when you speak with new prospects.

The truth is that you may be taken with certain features or benefits of your product/service, but that does not mean that your customer is equally interested in those same features or benefits. The only way that you can know what is truly helpful to your customers is to ask:

> *"(Customer name)*, I want to make sure that we continue providing what you need and want. What is it you like best about doing business with us? What else would you like to see?"

Another important question that almost no sales professionals use is to ask what you (your company, product or service) are doing wrong. If there is a problem, most customers will not tell you - they will simply leave and you will lose the customer. Head this off by periodically asking:

> *"(Customer name)*, I want to make sure that we continue providing what you need and want. What, if anything, is not working for you? What could we be doing better?"

Your customer may say that everything is wonderful in which case continue as you have been doing. Or your customer may tell you about some issues they've been having, and you will be able to solve the problems before they become so bad that your customer leaves.

Staying in touch with prospects and/or customers over time

Sometimes a prospect is indeed a qualified prospect, but there is a reason they must wait until a certain time has passed or a particular event has occurred in order to move forward, such as the beginning of a new budget year. If you have asked all the necessary questions and determined that the waiting time is indeed inevitable, you will want to stay in touch with that prospect until it is the right time for them to buy.

You may also have prospects you are very interested in turning into customers, but who are very loyal to their current vendor: despite your best efforts, you simply have not been able to get their agreement to try your product or service. If you continue to stay in touch over time, however, you may be able to build a relationship – or their vendor might make a mistake – that would enable you to really get in the door.

Perhaps you have customers who buy from you regularly. You want to maintain the relationship with these customers in such a way that you are not always calling them to say, "Are you ready to buy again?"

The solution to these scenarios is to send cards.

You might assume that I mean e-cards, which have become so popular and easy to generate, but prospects today are inundated with messages, and corporate spam filters may trap your email reminders, especially if they contain graphics. And unfortunately there are also now cases of computer viruses being circulated in the disguise of innocent e-card links, so spam filters are likely to become even tougher. When you send an e-card to a prospect there is no guarantee that they will actually see it.

The postal service, however, is a different story. If you send a card by first-class mail, your prospect *will* get it. In addition, cards make you stand out. Almost no one is sending cards these days - most are relying on email.

Sending a handwritten card to a prospect is a way of building a relationship that will grow over time. You can send thank you cards after a meeting or a phone call; a note of congratulations on specific events, such as if you have read or heard about your prospect - in a good way – in the news; holiday cards (for any holiday - even Halloween), birthday cards, and on and on.

I have consistently recommended to my clients that they stay in touch by cards. And I practice what I preach, too. For years I kept blank cards and stamps in my desk. Whenever I wanted to send a card they were there at hand. The only problem was that sometimes I'd run out of cards or stamps and then have to wait until I had a chance (in my busy schedule) to replace them.

Recently I've discovered a fully automated way to send cards to customers and prospects. The cards go out with a stamp on the envelope and in your own handwriting, once you file a simple 'Handwriting & Signature Form.' You can send postcards, greeting cards, and/or customized cards, and send them to one recipient at a time or to your entire address list, all for less than it would cost you to go to the store and buy cards.

I invite you to try this convenient networking and follow-up system by sending a complimentary card, courtesy of The Queen. Just go to www.thequeenscards.com, and click through to my free gift account for you!

Endless Follow-up

Sometimes sales representatives find themselves in the position of following-up and following-up and following-up... and never closing.

The way to eliminate this endless cycle is to always make sure that you are speaking only with qualified prospects. If you find yourself on the receiving end of endless call back requests use these scripts:

You:

> "(Prospect's name), I understand and am happy to call you back. Let me ask you a question though: What will have changed between now and *(whenever they said to call back)* that will enable us to move forward?"

OR

> "*(Prospect's name)*, we've been talking for awhile now, and you have indicated that we'd be able to help you *(fill in the benefit.)* I know that you're very busy and I don't want to waste your time or mine. I need to ask you, what is the probability we'll be able to work together in the next month?"

As I said in *Part I*, you are looking for the prospects who are looking for you, who are likely to buy (and preferably, come back regularly to buy more). At some point in the follow-up process, you may realize that a prospect no longer fits your *"Qualifying Parameters "*– they are no longer a prospect for you. Let them go.

Chapter 9. Closing Scripts

Before moving on to closing scripts I feel compelled to point out that it is imperative to listen carefully to your prospect and be constantly on the look-out for buying signals. Sometimes prospects are simply ready to buy. Prospects will say things like, "Wow, this is exactly what we need," or "This will solve so many problems," or "This is perfect." When that happens, stop talking. Your prospect doesn't need complicated scripts or more questions answered. They're ready. If you keep talking, you may muddy the waters and lose the sale.

> **...it is imperative to listen carefully to your prospect and be constantly on the look-out for buying signals.**

Unfortunately too many sales professionals miss these signals and miss orders that should have closed easily. If your prospect says to you, "Wow, this is exactly what we need," you have already closed. Stop selling. Now is the time to...

Ask for the order.

There is no substitute for coming right out and asking for the order.

You:

> "Let's get started, ok?"

> **OR**

> "Let's schedule your delivery for this week."

Alternative Choices - or: Assuming the Sale.

The alternation of options gives your prospect a choice and

assumes the answer is 'yes.' This helps to eliminate the possibility of a 'no.' (*The Appointment-Setting Mantra* in *Part III, Chapter 1* uses the alternative close.)

You:

> "Do you want the blue, or is green better?"

OR

> "Would you prefer delivery tomorrow or the day after?"

Everyone's Buying It.

You:

> "(On bigger orders) generally my customers want the (fill in the number) discount that comes with ordering (quantity). I assume you'd like that discount as well?"

Answer a Question with a Question.

If your prospect asks a 'buying question' - for example, "does it come in blue?" – always answer the question with a question of your own:

You:

> "Let me check for you. Shall I go ahead and schedule delivery if we have it?"

Another variation: If your prospect has asked for a discount:

You:

> "If I could get you a 10% discount would you place your order now?"

Let the Prospect Choose.

You:

> "Many of my customers start with the minimum order/ number/package of *(dollar amount)* and then realize they should have taken more...

"And some of my customers realize with an offer like this they really want to take the order/number/package up to the *(a higher dollar amount)* level…"

"And some of my other customers start right at the top with the premium order/number/package of *(dollar amount)* because it's such a great offer.

"Where are you with this?"

Take the Offer Away.

You:

"Well, you may be very right that this is not the right offer/solution/package for you. That's ok. Right now we have people/companies lining up around the block.

"The thing is that if you change your mind, I cannot guarantee that this particular offer/solution/package will still be available, and especially not at this price."

Sell Yourself.

If a prospect says to you that they believe they can get a better deal elsewhere:

You:

"If there was a better deal out there I'd be working for that company."

OR

"If you're looking for the best quality/service/guarantee/ results you won't find anything better than this, and I know that you will be happy with your decision here today."

Lowering the Price (a last resort).

The problem with this script is that far too many sales professionals are too willing to drop the price too quickly. Only do this if there is no other option - and never, ever give the full amount of the product/service for a lower price. You always need to eliminate something if you are going to drop the price.

You:

"I understand that you don't have it in your budget right now. You've said that if you had the budget you would want to move on this, correct?" *(Wait for the answer. The prospect must say 'yes' before you proceed.)*

THEN

"We might be able to do it without *(name two or three features that you can take out)*..."

OR

"We might be able to start with a smaller order of, *(smaller order than previously discussed)*..."

THEN

"I'll have to check it with my manager. If I can get the ok on this are you ready to proceed?" *(Again, wait for the answer. The prospect must say 'yes' before you proceed.)*

"That's great. Let me put you on hold for a moment while I go ask my manager." *(Put the prospect on hold for 30 seconds or so then come back on the line and close your sale.)*

Making A List...

You:

"You know what? Let's do this: Let's list all of the reason for going ahead now."

(Be sure to help your prospect out here. The idea is to get the focus off the negative objection and help them to start thinking positively. After you have helped listed a dozen or so advantages and they only have a few negatives:)

"You know, it was almost silly to make that list, and now that we have it's so obvious. This way you've got it in black and white - all the advantages that you will gain from owning this product/using this service. I know that you'll be happy with this decision. We can get this out to you on the 15th - or is the first of the month better?"

Adding Value (one more last resort).

Use this only as a last resort when other attempts have failed:

You:

"You really know how to drive a hard bargain. We can give you *(fill in an extra)* if you give me the go ahead right now. How is that?"

OR

"You really know how to drive a hard bargain, I like that. Just to show you how much I'm willing to give and how much I want your business, I'm going to give you my personal, direct line so that you don't ever have to worry about dealing with a switchboard or secretary or not getting through. Only my best clients have my direct dial. How do you want to pay for this? Credit card or company check?"

The Inept Sales Person

Use this only after you have received many 'no's.' Be as sincere as you can be with this script.

You:

"*(Prospect's name)*, before you go could you help me out for a moment? You see I truly believe in the value of this product/service. We help our customers in so many ways and yet I wasn't able to help you feel about it the way that I feel about it - and now I feel really badly that you'll have to keep using what you've been using/ doing what you've been doing and won't have all of the advantages of *(your product's/service's benefits)*.

"And this is how I earn my living and I'm worried that I'll make this same mistake again. Please tell me, what did I do wrong?"

(Listen to your prospect's answer. Then say:)

"That's it? You thought *(fill in what the prospect says)*? How dumb of me. No wonder you were concerned."

(Now go back and resell that particular point building value for all the features and benefits. Then say:)

"I'm glad we cleared that up. I'd hate to think that you were going to make a wrong decision simply because I hadn't fully explained the value of *(whatever point you were making)*. Do you want it in blue, or is green better?"

Tell a Story.

In this close you tell a story about someone who didn't let you help them and the dire consequences of that decision, for example:

You:

"Several months ago I was speaking with a business owner who at that time made the decision to go with another web design company instead of ours. Last week he called us in a panic. The web site had become a never-ending money pit and it still was not finished. So knowing our reputation for getting things done on time, he called to beg us to take over the project.

"We're happy to help him, however, by this point he's lost thousands of dollars that he should never have had to spend in the first place. So I've decided never to let that happen to another business owner that I speak with ever again. When would you like to get started? Next week or is the week after better?"

Sell Peace of Mind.

You:

"Wouldn't it be worth peace of mind knowing that you'll always have *(fill in with the benefits your prospect will gain)*?"

OR

"Wouldn't it be worth the peace of mind knowing that you're always secure with *(fill in with the benefits your prospect will gain)*?"

Chapter 10:
Words to Use and
Words to Avoid

What do the words that you use say about you? Do your words
support the impression that you wish to make? Do your words
support your sales message?

As a sales professional, you want to convey confidence and
authority. You always want your prospect or your customer to
see you as an expert in your field, as someone who is credible
and someone who is knowledgeable. Sometimes, the words you
use or the way you use them get in the way.

Have you ever started a conversation with a prospect or customer with the phrase "I'm just calling..."?

That little word "just" is an apology. It says that your call is not important and that what you have to say is not important. Delete it from your vocabulary immediately. Simply tell your prospects and customers why you are calling. That is enough.

"I believe that...."

"I think that...."

"I know...."

Who would you rather listen to? Someone who *believes* or *thinks* she knows something - or someone who simply knows it? The phrases "I believe" and "I think" detract from your message. They make you sound hesitant and unsure. Prospects are usually hesitant and unsure about buying from people who are hesitant and unsure.

"Once we have completed... we will hopefully achieve..."

Hopefully?

No one pays you to "hopefully" do something. They pay you to actually do it. Tell your prospects or customers what they will achieve or should expect to achieve.

Once you're ready to close the sale, mention your 'letter of agreement' or simply your 'agreement.' Avoid the word 'contract.' That word conjures up pictures of long, complicated, difficult paperwork, haggling attorneys and more expense. An 'agreement' is so much easier.

And speaking of 'easy,' always use 'easy.' Never, ever say that your product or service is 'difficult,' even if it is. In that case you can say, 'We'll make it easy for you.'

The same thing goes for the word 'simple.' Use it. Always avoid the words 'difficult' or 'hard.' Nobody wants to buy products or services that are difficult or hard.

Don't ever tell a prospect that you will 'try' to do something for them. Tell them that you 'will.' Who would you rather buy from: Someone who 'tries' or someone who comes through?

When asking your open-ended questions, simply ask: *who, how, what* and *why*. Do not say: 'May I ask you a question?' This question gives up your control of the conversation. With this question you are asking permission. You don't need permission to ask questions.

If you feel that you must ask, say, "Let me ask you a question." This phrasing assumes that asking the question is fine.

If a prospect asks you a question and you are unclear as to the answer, it is perfectly acceptable to say, "I'll find out." It's bad form to say, "I really am not sure."

If you hear a complaint from a prospect or customer (even if the complaint has nothing to do with you) say, "I'm sorry to hear that" or "I'm sorry that you had that experience." Do not say, "I can't believe that!"

Talk to your prospect about 'owning' your product. The word 'own' will help your prospect visualize herself with your product and using your product. 'Own' can be an emotional word, as in 'the pride of ownership.' You want your prospect to tap into that feeling. Conversely, avoid the word 'buy.'

You can also use the word 'invest' in place of the word 'buy.' For example: "When you invest in _____(*the product/service*)." Use the word 'investment' instead of 'price.' Another example: rather than saying, "The price is ___," say, "Your investment will be ____." This phrasing helps prospects see the value of your offering.

While there may certainly be individual cases where the above rules do not apply, paying attention to and being conscious of your choice of words will only strengthen your sales process.

It may take some time and practice before you are fully comfortable with these changes, but it will be time well spent when you see the difference in the way your customers and prospects respond. Your words are the building blocks that you use to motivate and persuade. Make sure they are the very best words that you have at your disposal.

Part V. In Conclusion: The Performance Model

I was never supposed to be an author, speaker and sales trainer. I was supposed to be a ballerina.

I grew up in Pittsburgh, PA. My mother has told me that when I was a small child I would constantly turn on the radio and dance. She said I had no sense of rhythm and so she enrolled me in ballet class. That was the beginning of a first career and a great passion.

As a child I danced with Pittsburgh Ballet Theater, always one of the child guests in Act I of *The Nutcracker*. As I grew older, it was the corps de ballet, Snowflake and Waltz of the Flowers. I was even the Sugar Plum Fairy a few times!

At 17 I moved to New York City to dance, and like every artist in the city, needed a day job. At first I waited on tables. Then I found something more lucrative and more fun - telemarketing.

An ad in "Backstage," the trade publication we would read to look for auditions, caught my attention. It was for a telemarketing company. They would hire actors because actors can read scripts. (Hiring tip: If you are looking for a part time telemarketer - hire an actor.) The job was calling high-level executives and setting new business appointments. I got the job and was really good at it. Who knew? Ballet dancers don't even talk.

Eventually the telemarketing company started to give me all the "hard leads," the Presidents, the CEOs, the people who "didn't take cold calls." I'd call them up, get them on the line, have a great conversation and set up the meeting. It was fun and it was easy.

Years later when I started my training and coaching business I thought that all that was necessary would be to show clients a system and help them write a good script and we would be done. Imagine my surprise upon discovering all of the human and psychological barriers people face when prospecting by telephone.

That sent me back to the basics, to think about not only the system and scripts but about thought processes and mindsets as well. I realized something fascinating: that everything that I know about telephone sales I learned in ballet class.

I want to share that knowledge with you via **The Performance Model.**

When you are speaking with a prospect on the telephone, you have about 10 seconds to grab and hold your prospect's attention. After that you probably will not have a second chance. You have a brief amount of time to tap into your prospect's psyche, feelings and desires, and all you really have to do this with is your voice and your words. In a fleeting moment you want to convey an idea, an impression, an emotion.

This is a performance. This does not mean that you must be an actor or that this is somehow phony: it simply means that if you think about your call in this manner then the preparatory steps are simple and easy to follow.

If you want your prospect to respond in a certain and favorable way you must be totally focused, at ease, comfortable, and one with your message. Part of being comfortable with and increasing your success is warming up for it. If you practice before you actually get on the telephone you will be in a much stronger position than if you simply "wing it." You must be prepared, know what you want to accomplish, and know how you plan to present yourself, your company and your product or service.

The Warm-Up

When you are a ballet dancer, the very first thing that you must do before any class, rehearsal or performance is warm up. You must stretch out and loosen up and get yourself ready and set up so that you can do what you need to do and so that you *do not hurt yourself.* In the same manner, your warm up for making sales calls is your preparation - everything that you need to do before you ever get on the telephone - so that you *do not hurt yourself!*

The warm-up for making sales calls includes understanding your market and crafting your script. It includes creating your introduction, outlining the questions you need to ask along with having an answer to every possible objection you may hear. You want to be so well prepared that your prospect never asks a question for which you do not have an answer. Then and only then is it time to get on the telephone.

Note: if a prospect does offer an objection that you have never heard before, do the best that you can at that moment. Then immediately after you hang up, write down the objection, and follow the recommendations in the *Introduction* about how to make sure you never are stumped by that objection again. In the same way, if a prospect asks a question for which you do not have an answer, say, "I do not know the answer to that but I can find out." Get the information you need and call the prospect back. If you do not understand the prospect's question or objection, ask for clarification. "Could you clarify that for me?" or "Would you be good enough to explain that further?" will work nicely.

The Rehearsal

Ballet dancers "take class," at least an hour-and-a-half ballet technique class every day, five or six days a week. A ballet class has a set structure with specific steps done in a specific order and with a built-in progression of difficulty of movement.

Everyone, whether a beginner or a professional dancer, follows the same class structure and does the same type of steps, with the advanced dancer doing variations of the steps that are more complicated than those of the beginner. Every day ballet dancers start *barre* (the warm-up) with *pliés*, followed by *tendus*, followed by *dégagés*. Everyone does this, every day. The teacher is there to watch and explain and give corrections. If a step does not work, if your balance is off or your "line" is wrong, or if you are falling out of a turn, the teacher is there to make corrections and help you improve.

When you get a correction, however, it is your job to implement it. Sometimes you might also ask a colleague for help, and you always, always watch yourself in the big mirror that is at the front of any dance studio. You critique yourself and work until you get it right. Dancing is a process: it does not happen overnight, but instead takes years of work and concentration.

Over the years of taking class every day, day after day, and repeating the same steps in the same order every day, day after day, a ballet dancer builds technique. Technique is habit. You practice the same steps over and over again until you no longer have to think about them. It is just second nature, a part of you. The technique is simply there.

Your rehearsal process for making sales calls will work in the same manner. When you rehearse your script over and over you are building your technique - the habits that will get you successfully through your calls. If you are prepared, and you work with the material and rehearse it, your telephone approach and telephone manner will simply become second nature. You will not have to stop and think when a prospect offers an objection. You will know the answer - it will just come out. By the time you start calling you will almost be on auto-pilot. You will know what you want to say and how you are going to say it. That is why we sales trainers are so fond of role-playing. It is rehearsal.

Building a solid calling technique has another great advantage. When you are having a good day, it is very easy to be "on." Technique will give you a way to get yourself "on" when you are having a bad day. Building technique gives you a process to pull yourself together and get to where you need to be to do your work. That "auto-pilot" process will kick in, allowing you to leave your bad day behind.

I think about a sales call the same way I think about a dance performance. Any series of steps or sequence of movement has its own phrasing and timing. As a dancer I have to decide which steps are held, which are emphasized, which are moved through quickly, what it is that I want my audience to see and to feel. This discovery is part of the rehearsal process.

In your telephone work you need to decide what it is that you want your prospect to hear and also to feel. How will you get them to hear and feel what you want them to hear and feel? Which words will you emphasize? Which words will you move through quickly? This is why working with a tape recorder and also practicing with friends or colleagues is so valuable.

Your goal is to draw your listener into your performance, to be so one with the material, focused and committed, that your prospect hears and responds favorably to what you are saying.

The supreme test for a ballerina is 32 *fouettés*. A *fouetté* is a 360-degree turn on one leg, performed without putting the other leg down, "on your toes," without traveling from the spot on the floor where you start. In the last act of the great classical ballets such as *Swan Lake* or *Giselle*, there is always a duet for the two principal dancers. This is called the *Grand Pas de Deux*. This dance is a formula dance, and as part of that formula the ballerina must perform 32 *fouettés*. Your audience counts along, so if you only perform 31 *fouettés* they know. Some of them will sneer at you later.

It is the common wisdom that in order to "nail" 32 *fouettés* on stage you have to be able to do 64 *fouettés* in class. That is: do 64 turns in a row, on one leg, "on your toes," without putting the other leg down and without traveling from the spot on the floor where you start.

This is how you learn how to do 64 *fouettés*: everyone spreads out in the dance studio facing the big mirror in the front, and the accompanist starts to play. The music is always a kind of circus-like music with a very driving rhythm. You begin to do *fouettés* and you perform one or two and then you fall down. You get up, you perform another one or two *fouettés*, and then you fall down. You get back up, you perform another one or two *fouettés*, and then you fall down. Pretty soon, before you know it, you are performing three or four *fouettés* - and then you fall down. That is how it works.

But what is really marvelous and exciting about this entire process is that if you keep practicing, keep working on your *fouettés* and perfecting your technique - you get better, it gets easier and one day you can do it: 32 – or 64 – *fouettés*.

It works exactly the same way with selling by phone. If you keep working on your calls and your scripts and delivery, you get better, it gets easier and you can do it.

Whether it is performing *fouettés* or making sales calls, no one is simply born knowing how to do it perfectly. Ballet dancers must be tenacious, dedicated, disciplined and hard-working. Training a ballet dancer takes many, many years. Fortunately, learning to sell by phone is a much shorter process than either learning to perform 32 *fouettés* or becoming a professional ballet dancer. It does, however, require knowledge, patience and persistence.

This program is only a jumping off point. If you are doing something that works for you - keep doing it. If, after you have worked in a certain way for a while, an approach that you are using does not bring the success you want - try something new. Give it some thought, ask a colleague, read books, take seminars... The point is that you do not quit. You fall down; you get up and perform the steps again.

The Performance

When you are dancing your focus must always be "in the moment" - you are only thinking about what you are doing right then. You are not looking at the past; you are not looking into the future. You are only in the present.

If you are performing and you make a misstep, you deal with it at that moment, and then you go on. This is called focus. Your audience doesn't care that you've made a misstep – they probably don't even notice. Once that step is finished you are on to the next without looking back. The important part is that you stay in the moment, deal with what is happening in the moment, and continue to move forward. If you allow yourself to hold onto the mistake or to feelings about the mistake, you will probably simply make more mistakes.

Sometimes certain steps or certain parts of the choreography can be extremely difficult. If you are anxious about a difficult step that comes later in the choreography, you cannot allow your anxiety about that difficult step to make you lose focus and misstep on the parts that are not as difficult.

This works exactly the same way in sports and in many areas of life, including making telephone sales.

When making sales calls, you must be there, in that moment, with the person with whom you are speaking. If you have had a problem with an earlier call, you must let go of that problem and the feelings you may have about it. If you are anxious about being able to schedule a meeting or about the meeting itself, you need to do the work to reduce your anxiety.

The best way to do that is to be aware of your negative internal dialogue. You do have control of your thoughts and it is your choice to move forward or to hang onto the bad feelings created by your thoughts. Stay in the moment. Don't worry about the future. Don't hold on to the past. Focus on what is happening right now and only on what is happening right now. If you move from moment to moment in this manner, your calls will be much easier and far less stressful.

You may find that you are nervous, afraid or anxious when you first start making introductory calls, and that is perfectly normal - it is called stage fright. In the world of ballet, you take class every day, day after day, week after week, year after year, polishing and perfecting your technique. And it is technique that gets you through stage fright.

The more you perform the easier it gets. If you build a solid calling technique it will get you through your calling anxiety. And as you continue to make calls your anxiety and stage fright will diminish - I promise.

Sales Resource Guide

The Queen of Cold Calling Recommends:

For New Sales Hires:

Prospecting University: a turnkey solution for decreasing sales representative turnover while increasing sales.

Weiss Communications
Phone: 866-405-8212
E-mail marlene@wendyweiss.com or tamara@wendyweiss.com, or
visit us at www.wendyweiss.com/prospectinguniversity

***

Referral System:

The Ultimate Referral and Follow-up System: follow-up with prospects, build strong relationships and generate boundless referrals, http://www.thequeenscards.com.

***

Prospecting Software:

Klpz, by Contact Science, is web-based software specifically designed to enable any Best Practices for any telephone prospecting program - cold calling, lead follow up or customer up sell. The Klpz approach is easy for field sales reps to operate, will double their productivity and will automatically generate management reports on their prospecting activity. Find out more about Klpz at 214-483-5800. Ask for your complimentary *Queen's Calculator* to use in determining how many targets you can effectively call each year. www.contactscience.com

***

CRM System:

SalesNexus is online customer relationship management (CRM) with powerful email marketing built-in. SalesNexus enables sales teams from 5 to 200 to increase quality leads, manage more opportunities effectively and close more business.

Contact Cheryl Curtis at 800-862-0134 x105, email sales@salesnexus.com or visit http://www.wendyweiss.com/nexus. Mention, "*The Queen* sent me" to receive a free one month trial of the software.

***

Virtual Assistants:

Team Double-Click®: In these tough economic times it can be quite difficult for a business owner to gain market share and still get all of their daily administrative tasks done alone. Wouldn't it be great if you had a little help? Don't just dream about taking your business to the next level. Make it happen!

Team Double-Click® offers full service virtual assistant services. Tell them *The Queen* sent you and get 2 free hours of virtual assistant services with your first 10 billed hours. 888-827-9129 http://www.wendyweiss. com/TDC .

***

LinkedIn and Web 2.0:

Your Profile Now!® helps you create a great profile for tremendous personal branding.

Professional LinkedIn® profiles that will allow you to be found! Professional profile completed according to the current SEO and LinkedIn® rules.
Professional profile that gets you to prominent search levels on Yahoo® and Google®.
Your Profile Now!® can create a professional profile in One Week or Less.

Tell them, "*The Queen* Sent Me" for a 10% discount.

678-568-2976, info@YourProfileNow.com

www.JimBrowning.us
www.YourProfileNow.com

***

TopSalesExperts.com:

Top Sales Experts delivers the most successful, innovative and inspiring collection of global professional sales experts (including *The Queen*) ever assembled in one location. *TSE's VIP Zone* offers valuable support for increased opportunities and sales every day. Become a VIP member for access to virtual Masterclasses, eBooks, interactive assessments, interviews with sales gurus, and much more. http://www.queenofcoldcalling.com/member

Wendy Weiss, The Queen of Cold Calling, is an author, speaker, sales trainer, and sales coach. She is recognized as one of the leading authorities on lead generation, cold calling and new business development and she helps clients speed up their sales cycle, reach more prospects directly and generate more sales revenue. Her clients include Avon Products, ADP, Sprint and thousands of entrepreneurs throughout the country.

Ms. Weiss has been featured in the New York Times, BusinessWeek, Entrepreneur Magazine, Selling Power, Sales & Marketing Management and various other business and sales publications. She is the author of the book, Cold Calling for Women and the recently released, 101 Cold Calling Tips for Building New Customers in a Down Economy. She is also a featured author in two recently released books, Masters of Sales and Top Dog Sales Secrets.

Wendy is also a former ballet dancer who believes that everything she knows in life she learned in ballet class.